# THE SPELL OF THE HORSE

## Stories of Healing and Personal Transformation with Nature's Finest Teachers

Pam Billinge

blackbird

First Published in 2017 by Blackbird Digital Books
Blackbird Digital Books
2/25 Earls Terrace
London W8 6LP
1 2 3 4 5 6 7 8 9 10 11 12
www.blackbird-books.com
Copyright © Pam Billinge 2017
This edition published December 2022
Pam Billinge has asserted her right to be identified as the author of this work.
A CIP catalogue record for this book is available from the British Library
ISBN 978-1-8382786-7-0
Cover design by http://mecob.co.uk/

## Praise for *The Spell of the Horse*

*'Pam Billinge writes with a wonderful beauty.'*
Liz Loves Books

*'Honest, authentic and full of wisdom.'* Goodreads
*'Beautifully-written, finely-constructed, humanely-told. I
have read (and written) many books about leadership
development, and this is one of the best.'* Jonathan Gosling,
Emeritus Professor of Leadership, University of Exeter and
Director of Pelumbra Ltd

*'This book will repay the few hours it will take you to read
it many times over.'* Goodreads

*'Not just for horse lovers but for anyone interested in
finding sustainable ways to overcome personal challenges.'*
Goodreads

*'Having spent several years training as a counsellor, I have
learnt more about the human mind and spirit from just
reading this book.'* Amazon reader

*'Her special affinity and deep respect for horses shines
through with every well-written word and every emotional
connection.'* Jaffa Reads Too

*This book is dedicated to my brothers Gordon and Colin,
my mum Brenda, my dad Roy and my stepfather Lorenz*

# Contents

Introduction  1

1  This Horse Changed my Life  5

2  Carabella: The Spell is Cast  12

3  Delilah: The Language of the Herd Revealed  17

4  Presence and Connecting with the Self  23

5  Gemma: Tragedy and Loss of Self  29

6  You Can't Fool a Horse  35

7  After Gemma  39

8  Winston: Loss Unfolding  42

9  Mum: Making up Lost Time  46

10 Winston: Teaching Me to Choose Courage  52

11 Accepting the Need to Change  57

12 Building Resilience  62

13 Coop: Chosen by a Horse  65

14 With Coop: Healed by Peacefulness  69

15 The Burnout Trap  74

16 Coop's Lesson in Honesty  81

17 Emotions – Friend not Foe  84

18 Emotions at Work  88

19 Coop: The Challenge of Trusting  94

20 Vulnerability and Change  98

21 Coop's Inspiration: Daring to Dream  102

22 Coop: Saying Goodbye  107

23 Committing to Purpose  110

24 Seen by a Horse  112

25 A Team Moves From Fear to Authenticity  117

26 Ruby: A Heart Connection  121

27 Staying on Course  125

28 Victim No More  130

29 The Power of Positive Thinking  134

30 Committing to Purpose  138

31 Gordon  144

32 Finding Joy Amongst Grief  149

33 Courage to Grieve  152

34 Horses: Our Spiritual Guides  157

35 Being With What Is  162

36 Spirit as Guide  167

37 Winning Means Losing  171

38 How Horses Teach Us Compassion 177

39 Following Joy  179

40 Living the Dream  184

41 Healing Through Forgiveness  190

Acknowledgements  206

About the Author  208

# *Introduction*

The kind of work I do is sometimes called equine assisted learning, coaching or psychotherapy. I believe, however, that it is me who assists the horses, not the other way around. So I prefer to describe my approach as being 'horse-led'. My methods have grown from real personal experience and making sense of what I see happening again and again between horse and human, as well as being built on the foundations of my professional training and experience as a psychotherapist, leadership coach and relational horsemanship specialist. I support all kinds of people: from chief executives of global organisations, to corporate teams, through to extraordinary young people who struggle to learn and fit in with what society expects of them. Mindful encounters with horses have transformed many lives before my eyes.

At the age of 52 my elder brother Gordon died suddenly. Neither the great medical breakthroughs of our time, nor my desperate prayers, could save him from the infection which took him in days. Afterwards, I found comfort with my herd, with them I could allow my emotions to be what they were.

One morning in early April with birdsong in my ears and that damp, sweet, scent that promises spring in the air, I led two of my horses, Winston and Ruby, out of the stable yard down the long grassy track to their paddock at the edge of the farm. I pushed the five-bar gate open and let them loose. They spun on their heels and galloped, hooves flying, to the far end of the pasture where the lushest grass was to be found.

I paused to watch them settle to their grazing in the distance, toy figures against the blossom frothing white against the blue sky. My brother had loved mornings like this. Grief jolted me, its dark shadow smothering the brightness. Far away, Ruby lifted her head high, curving her neck to look at me. She hesitated, alert, then sprung into a canter, a dew trail marking her path towards me. Ruby stood with me, her soft muzzle on my arms, tickling my wet, salty face with her whiskers, as if inhaling my sadness. She let me sink into her and stayed until I took my arms from around her and hugged myself. Then she drifted and trotted back to where she had left her field mate grazing.

Ruby had come when I needed her, sensing it from a long way. I understood then, with absolute certainty, that the ability of the horse to sense emotion, energy and spirit is beyond what most of the human world realises. This is why their impact on us can be so instant, so consistently positive, so transformational.

There is no mistake – these incredible creatures can tune into the silent vibration of a breaking heart from afar.

Horses do not lie. Nor do they worry about hurting our feelings or denting our pride. Carabella, Delilah, Gemma, Winston, Coop, Ruby, Dawn and Ellie: they have led me on an incredible journey and helped me to become who I am today. I didn't always like what they told me but it was always what I needed to hear. In 2008 I found the courage to trust what they had been showing me for some years – that they had a significant contribution to make to the opening of our consciousness and to my work as a therapist and coach.

My hope is that with this book you will be able to share in the inspiration and insights they have given me, and many others. Universally relevant lessons about managing anxiety; surviving bereavement; the importance of being calm, present and mindful; of learning to let go of fear and find courage; of living with joy and purpose and being true to your spirit.

You may be curious about my methods when I work with horses and my clients developmentally, or you might be seeking to deepen your understanding of the nature and behaviour of horses. Perhaps you are looking for solutions to a difficult situation in your own life. As you read, you might even find answers to questions you didn't know you wanted to ask. For this is the Spell of the Horse, and once you have fallen under it, anything can happen. Horses can inspire you to re-evaluate your own life, invest in your real, essential self and take the first confident steps towards truth, peace and purpose. With them, by learning to listen to your inner wisdom, without overthinking dilemmas, you can allow the right thing to happen in your life rather than trying to force it.

If horses are part of your life you may find that this book helps you to deepen your relationship with them and understand what might go wrong between you from time to time. If you don't have contact with these beautiful animals then perhaps you might wish to by the time you finish reading.

I would like to thank all my clients for helping me to find my path while I have helped them to find theirs. The characters and their stories in this book, other than my own, are fictional, but the encounters that take place with the horses are true to real events.

# 1

## *This Horse Changed my Life*

It was a sunny and warm day in July when even the bees pollinating the clover seemed sleepy. The 12-year-old girl greeted me and my co-therapist Lindsay with a bespectacled, eager smile.

Alice was bright with a remarkable intellect. But she was also lost and lonely. She struggled to make friends or to interact with those around her. Particularly her peers. As we sat together in the grass for our initial discussion, she talked about her isolation in a resigned, matter of fact way. Her world was closed; she was at best ignored or at worst bullied at school. She had stopped wanting to go at all.

'Which horse do I get?' she asked as we walked down the track to the paddocks.

'You get to choose,' I said.

She picked the first pony we came to, Obe, a gentle and docile veteran with a pearlescent sheen to his coat. When she got to about four feet from him he slowly but determinedly turned away, keeping the same distance between them as she advanced towards him.

The child shrugged her shoulders. 'He doesn't seem to like me ... shall I try that brown one over there?' pointing to Barney who grazed a short distance away.

I nodded permission but exactly the same thing happened. She frowned. 'Hmm. They really don't seem to like me, do they?' She paused. 'What about this one?'

Her cheerfulness had gone, and her enthusiasm with it, when she stepped hesitantly towards Max. He, too, drifted away from her. This place of rejection felt familiar for her. By now some time had passed and I noticed that we only had 10 minutes of the session left.

'OK!' she announced bravely. 'This is definitely my last attempt! I'll see if this one likes me.'

I opened the gate for her into the next paddock where a big white horse with brown patches and a black and white mane was meandering. This was my horse, Winston. I worked hard to let go of my need for Alice to have a positive experience but didn't quite manage it.

'This horse likes his tummy being scratched,' I whispered as she walked tentatively towards him.

This time, Winston didn't move away. He looked up at the girl from his grazing, then put his head down again to eat some more. Alice managed to make it to his rather round belly and without hesitation set about scratching vigorously with both tiny hands.

Winston stretched his muzzle up towards the sky, extending his strong neck. 'More please!' the expression on his face said as his top lip stiffened and curled, revealing his very large teeth and pink gums. The child broke into peals of laughter. And thus they got acquainted, the girl gleeful and the horse showing his appreciation in his comical way. The deal was done. They were friends. Was this horse of mine the first friend that she had ever made, I wondered.

A week later Alice chose to work with Winston again. She had spent the week reading about horses and reeled off to me her newly acquired and already sophisticated grasp of equine psychology and behaviour as we walked down to the paddock. As soon as he saw her, Winston's ears flicked forwards with interest. After some initial belly scratching, however, he quickly lost interest in his young companion and meandered off to graze. Alice tried to capture his interest a couple of times to no avail.

'He doesn't like me anymore. It's like when I try to get my friends to play with me at school. They always go off and do other things,' she said, her head bowed.

'What game would you most like to play with your friends?' I asked.

'I'd like them to come round to my house and build Lego or do painting and stuff like that. Or ride our bikes.'

'So let's build something that we'll pretend is your house, and your job is going to be to get Winnie to come and join you there. How does that sound?'

'Cool!'

So we put four poles, the sort you build show jumps out of, in a square shape on the ground, forming a large box.

'It needs to be bigger than that if it's my house! And if Winnie is going to get into it. He is quite big you know!' she instructed, as if I had not noticed. She was very clear on what she wanted.

The box built, I asked her what she had learned that week about horses that might help her invite him into her 'house'.

She thought out loud. 'Er, well, they like food. But there is grass everywhere, so that won't help. They also like friends – they live in a herd. That might be useful. They also sleep on three legs, which is fine, 'cause he can do that in the box too …' she worked her way through all her horse facts, one by one.

'And how would you approach him, if he was one of your friends who you were inviting to come and play?'

'Well, I would go and knock on his door and ask him if he wanted to play out.'

'And do your friends usually come when you do that?'

'Hmm no, they usually don't.'

'So what might tempt your friends or Winston to come?

How could you make the offer more interesting?'

'OK, well, I suppose I could tell them what we were going to do. And I could have some cake or biscuits as well to give them.'

'So does that give you some ideas for what you might do with Winnie?'

'Yes!'

She skipped excitedly down the paddock to invite Winston to go and play in her house.

'Come on Winnie, come and play! she said, waving her arms animatedly as she approached him. 'We're going to play with Lego, and I have got cakes and stuff for you! And you can bring your friends; there is loads of room! We're all going to be in a herd together. You can even sleep on three legs if you like!'

Each time she offered an incentive, her arms flailed round even more excitedly, her voice got louder and her enthusiasm quickly filled the whole paddock such was its intensity.

To her surprise, Winston's interest was piqued.

'Yay!' she cried. 'Come on! You know you want to come! Hurry up before the others eat all the cake! Hurry up!'

By now, she was beside him with her fingers and palm resting lightly on his muscular shoulder. Then she swung to face towards her 'house' and skipped forwards. The huge horse followed gently and willingly, his head lowered in relaxation. At the threshold of the box marked out on the ground Alice stepped decisively over the nearest pole. The horse followed her so they were both standing inside the imagined walls of her bedroom.

'Good boy!' she cooed, running bent fingers back and forth across his tummy. 'Now you can go to sleep if you like!'

Winston remained wakeful and stood quietly until her vigorous rubbing softened into a stroke. After a while, he lifted one foot at a time over the make-believe boundary in front of him and put his head down to graze. The work for that day was done.

'Alice, well done! How was that? What did you learn?' I asked.

'That was amazing! I love Winnie so much! I learned that he likes it when I scratch him. And he will come with me if he wants to.'

'And what did you do differently, do you think, which made him want to come with you?'

'Hmm, I suppose I told him about all the great stuff we were going to do, things I knew he would like to do.'

'And how will what you learned help you when you go to invite your human friends to play?'

She fell silent and reflected some more. 'I suppose I have to believe that they will want to come and play with me when I ask them.'

Alice went home with a bounce in her step. We met a third time, and then a week after that it was time for her fourth and final visit.

Alice again chose Winston as her playmate for the day. Her confidence had grown exponentially and it was touching to see this slight person being so comfortable alongside the copious horse who was showing genuine fondness for his new partner.

Alice chose to work in the arena. She set out a series of obstacles, representing the challenges in her life, which she would need to negotiate with Winston. He would be at liberty with no rope or halter on. The complexity of the course she built for him was arresting.

'OK, so the horse will gallop round the arena following me, then I will ask him to stop and stand in that spot over there, then trot round this cone in a circle, then gallop the other way, then zigzag round these poles, jump the jump, and then we are finished.'

Alice ambled over to the horse who had been waiting ears pointed sharply forwards watching her every move intently.

'Come on, Winnie, let's go!' Alice set off at a run, and to my astonishment, he followed and off they went in a cloud of dust.

Soon, the child was standing in the centre of the arena, her short arms energetically directing the horse whose attention never wavered from her. He galloped round in perhaps the most beautiful shape I had ever seen – noble, proud, strong, powerful, totally engaged with this small person. 'Stop!' Alice shouted as Winnie approached the spot on the course where they had to stand together. And to my amazement the horse slid to a stop beside her. It was incredible to witness.

Afterwards, Alice, Lindsay and I sat at a picnic table outside the arena. Winnie grazed next to Alice.

'Is there anything you would like to say to, or about, Winnie?' Lindsay asked gently.

There was no real need for any other words. The child was thoughtful for a moment. Then placing her plump hand gently on the flank of the horse she said, 'This horse changed my life. Because he did not judge me. So I did not judge him.'

Profound words from such a young person who had understood what it was to give and receive unconditional regard. I was humbled. My horse had changed this girl's life. I knew he had also changed mine. I felt an even deeper respect for him. And in this moment as well as connecting in a new way to Winston, I did so, too, with myself and my direction. This *was* right. I was on my path. This was no longer a dream; it was my reality.

A year earlier, I would scarcely have believed it was possible that I would be working in this way. But now that my purpose was clear, I could see how I had slowly been finding it these past years, without even realising that I was necessarily looking for it. Perhaps, I wondered, *it* had been finding *me*.

Horses had led me to this day, step by step, revealing their secrets and their infinite wisdom a little at a time.

## 2

## *Carabella: The Spell is Cast*

### *Andalusia, 1990*

I was in my late twenties – mending a broken heart. The man I loved, the man whose children I had wanted, who made me feel like a girl and a goddess all at once, did not want to marry me. So I had ended it. Every cell of my being had been intoxicated with him, his scent, his sensual touch and joie de vivre. When our relationship finished, it seemed like my soul had died too.

To escape from the life that I had known with him at its centre, I had taken a new job – a big promotion bringing an impressive salary and company car. I moved from London to Lancashire. But it was stressful work in a toxic environment. And there up in the North, I had no friends. No family nearby. I was a fish out of water. My loneliness kept me awake at night, and I wondered how I would ever come alive again.

At the end of the working day, I would climb into my car and my professional façade would crumble. Often, I didn't make it home before my body broke under the weight of my tears and I would pull into a lay-by until they had run dry.

Five months after my move up to Lancashire, I felt ready to lift myself out of my sadness. I decided to take the holiday of a lifetime. It was also the first step on an important life journey to which I was oblivious at the time. One which would later help me through loss, desperation and isolation, and through which I would find joy, peace and a purpose that I would never have thought possible.

I was to spend a week riding in Las Alpujarras, a mountainous region in Southern Spain. I was to reconnect with two happy memories – riding lessons taken as a teenager and a year spent studying and working in Spain as part of my degree.

I arrived late in the evening at Malaga airport with the four other people taking the same holiday. We were met by a tanned young Scottish woman who would also be our guide through the mountains. Aboard an old minibus we wound our way up and up from the coast road, our route twisting and winding through the night. As we arrived at the 'finca' whose whitewashed walls glowed out of the thick darkness, I was mystified by the melodious, mysterious song of a nightingale. The warm air was fragrant from the blossoming olive, orange and lemon groves surrounding the farmhouse. I knew already that this was going to be an adventure I would never forget.

We rode 20 or 30 miles a day from one hamlet to the next, through verdant gorges, across high-altitude pastures watered by the melting snow, and along rocky tracks carved into the exposed flanks of the mountains. The horses were big, strong Andalusians with fluid manes and tails and gentle natures. We carried one change of clean clothes and basic toiletries in our saddlebags. All trappings of my high-flying career were left behind.

Sometimes we lodged in basic guest houses and other times with families in their humble, rural homes. One family we stayed with had mosquito net instead of glass in some of the windows and we slept on mattresses made by hand from knotted rags. Meals were cooked over a single open fire in the corner of a sparse, bare kitchen, one dish at a time. Our wine was made locally and served from old Coca-Cola bottles. The family lived on the first floor of the property and their animals on the ground floor, which was accessed from the cobbled street via a huge pair of barn doors painted white. Mules, goats, chickens, a sheep and its lambs were all crowded in together, and our horses joined them too for the night. The simplicity of the lives of our hosts left me uncomfortable when I remembered the brand new company car sitting on my driveway. After a long day in the saddle, enveloped by the bountiful hospitality of these poor, sun and wind-burned people, I fell asleep to the muffled sounds of the animals beneath. I could not remember such deep contentment or gratitude.

We were generally alone on our route excepting an occasional farmworker, with two or three mules in tow, disappearing beneath the untidy bundles of crops tied onto their backs. The ancient tracks we rode were at times treacherous with loose stones and slippery moss stealing our tread and often so steep that we had to get off and lead our horses. Scrambling up or down on hands, knees and bottoms with half a ton of horse behind was arduous. One of the descents was particularly extreme, with the path slashed in a colossal zigzag from the ridge of the mountain through swathes of rough scree down to a verdant gorge below. The ground fell away from the track so abruptly I didn't dare peep over the edge but kept my eyes fixed on the path in front, focussing on one step at a time. I had no other option than to trust my horse Carabella not to stand on me or spook and tip me into the abyss at my side.

The challenging terrain of the hills yielded through corridors of bright yellow gorse to water meadows where the scent of the fresh herbs crushed beneath the horses' hooves drifted deliciously around us. Streams gurgled clean and clear across smoothed shiny grey pebbles and at one crossing the water lapped the horses' round bellies and splashed the soles of our boots. I wanted to absorb every second of this intoxicating experience.

### *The spell of the horse*

Most of all though it was this horse, Carabella, who inhabited my every moment. She was mine, for the week. A kind, huge, dark brown mare with black mane and tail. Strong, quiet and athletic. I sensed that she would keep me safe. I had been smitten with the idea of horses and ponies for as long as I could remember and received sporadic riding lessons as a child. But I'd never grown so close to a horse, living alongside one day-to-day. Now I knew how it could be to journey in partnership with such a creature.

With each stride that Carabella took, she brought me more and more into the moment. My head emptied little by little of the worries of work and the self-recrimination about my failed relationship which preyed on me as I tried to make sense of the rejection. And as this happened, astride and alongside this horse, pleasure had returned without me even noticing it. My body and soul were moving to a different rhythm. The self-pity had gone. My vitality was back. I was thankful for every breath I took in this incredible world. I was under the Spell, the Spell of the Horse. Healing had commenced.

When the week ended and it was time to go home, I sat in the straw beside Carabella for my final hour with her. I could hardly bear to say goodbye. Yet mixed with the sadness, there was a frisson of hope and excitement. There was a 'maybe' taking shape in my consciousness that I had never dared to entertain. I knew this was the beginning of a story and not the end. But I never imagined how it would unfold. How this new connection with horses would help me through some dark days, liberating me into a new purpose, where I would help others to do the same on their own life trajectory.

## 3

## *Delilah: The Language of the Herd Revealed*

### *Lancashire, 1990*

Several weeks after my holiday in Spain with Carabella, I started having riding lessons near to my home in Lancashire. I had made few friends since my relocation, so learning to ride properly seemed the perfect solution.

The process was disappointing in comparison. I would arrive to be presented with a horse already wearing saddle and bridle and be drilled through my lesson in the indoor arena by a rather regimental teacher. It was nothing like the experience I had enjoyed with Carabella during my journey in the Spanish mountains.

Then, one day, a new horse was brought out for me to ride. She was a dark chestnut colour with striking flaxen mane and tail. Curiously, she had one blue eye and one brown eye. When I climbed onto her broad back, I realised she was different to the others. She responded sensitively to what I asked of her. I guessed that she had not been numbed by years of teaching novices on her back. At the end of the lesson, I didn't want to climb down; I felt like I belonged with her.

'What's her name?' I asked the man who ran the stables.

'Delilah,' he said. 'And she's for sale.'

Several days later, I had parted with far too much money for what this horse was worth and found myself standing, in a trance-like state, with my arms folded on top of her stable door, gazing in on her.

'She's mine,' was all I could think. 'At last I have my own pony.'

Even in the gloom of the poorly lit, shabby stable, her mane and tail glistened like spun silk as she watched me suspiciously. Threads of silver, gold, grey, white, ginger, black and yellow fell opulently about her rump. If I had known anything about horses, which I didn't, I would have recognised that other than her beautiful hair, this mare was in poor shape. Her coat was dull and lacklustre, her ribs showed. But in spite of her aloofness, something had drawn me to her. Perhaps I recognised that she needed me as much as I her. Had I not been so naïve, I would also have known that she was not 12 years old as the owner of the yard had told me, but well over 20. He must have relished taking my thousands off me when on the open market she was worth little more than meat money.

But Delilah provided an antidote to the highly stressful job in which I found myself. I poured energy, love and time into her. Over the months, she responded. Her eyes brightened, and a lustre was born in her coat as she filled out on good food. I had moved her from the riding school where I had bought her to a farm near the cottage where I lived. It was a rough and ready place, a former dairy, but the horses who were kept there roamed across many acres of paddocks as one big herd, unlike the other, more elegant, equestrian yards in the area. There the horses seemed to spend most of their time in clean stables wrapped in expensive rugs. No mud to be seen. That was not what I wanted for my horse. I wanted to see her run free. In time her trust for me grew and then, thrillingly, she would seek me out. She would rest her head against my chest while I rubbed behind her ears, and run to meet me at the gate. She looked after me, the novice rider, when we rode out on the lanes and trails.

Even the gruelling toil of the winter months hardly dulled my delight at this new world I had discovered. I would shed my business suit and don jeans, boots and sweater and make my way to the stables. There, the pressures and worries of organisational politics vaporised as I inhaled the intoxicating scent of warm horse in the straw-bedded stable where she would spend the night in winter. Like Carabella had done, Delilah knew how to bring me into the moment, such that the anxieties of the day faded away, for a few hours at least so that my soul was restored.

### *Bad news*

In the middle of our third winter together, I noticed changes in Delilah's health. The vet was called, and after tests were carried out, he diagnosed bowel cancer. 'Typical of these old horses.' I reeled with shock. I thought she was younger and in her prime. I had been well and truly duped. Nothing could be done other than to make her comfortable for as long as we could.

Delilah needed 100 prednisolone tablets twice a day. I would count them out one dose at a time into sandwich bags on a Sunday evening. Then each night I would carefully embed each dose of 100 into a lavishly buttered sandwich. It was the best way I found of getting her to eat them. It was hard to believe that she was dying. She still looked so well, so beautiful, her strong neck, shoulders and rump muscled proudly. She had become a stunning horse in the time that she had been with me, and I had learned that caring for a horse till it shines with health, power and vigour is like creating the finest, living masterpiece in the world.

By May, Delilah seemed increasingly uncomfortable, and I would find her lying down in the field resting more often than I knew was normal. I had to accept that, out of love for her, a decision had to be made. I had to find the courage to end this life, which was now so much part of mine and a source of such gladness. One morning, she ambled to meet me at the gate. When she laid her head gently on my chest for her ears to be rubbed, I could not deny that the look in her eye had changed. I did not want her to suffer. I braced myself and rang the vet. 'Sooner rather than later,' I said. 'OK, how about tomorrow, I can do 3.30pm.'

### *Making the moments matter*

It was a beautiful May morning, several days before my birthday. I took the day off work, rose early and made up a picnic hamper with food and drink. I didn't know how I would get through the day but I was going to make every second with her count. So although I was now engaged to be married I would face it alone. I would be there, with Delilah, for what was to come. I didn't want anyone else spoiling it for me. Perhaps I should have been more attuned, then, to this whispered instinct about my future husband.

I took a rug from the cupboard, which I was soon spreading in the buttercups and fragrant green grass. I sat out with Delilah in the paddock, watching her silently, soaking in the sight of her. In spite of my grief it was a day of rich memories. Listening and counting the rhythm as she chewed the grass and noticing the sweetness of it on her breath. I didn't groom her; she didn't ask for it. But being alongside her was enough. That was what I had always loved, feeling her sturdy presence close by. That was what I was going to miss.

The vet came to administer the injection. I had chosen a discrete spot outside the main field. It was spring, and the rest of the herd were grazing in the bottom pasture, far away from the farmyard. He warned me that it would be difficult to witness, but I wanted to stay. Leaving her was not an option.

### The herd says good bye

Delilah fell to the ground and I dropped to my knees beside her. Her neck felt strong and warm under my hand as I murmured sweet words of thanks and love. Then I heard a low rumble of thunder. The noise grew in volume. It was the sound of pounding hooves. The entire herd of twenty or thirty horses came into view, galloping as one through a gap in the hedgerow behind which lay the acres of spring and summer grazing. Greys, bays, dapples, chestnuts mingling and merging like a herd of wild horses running out on the plain, legs lost in the dust they made, manes and tails tossing. The herd slid to a standstill dramatically and lined up along the fence in front of me, mostly still but stirring slightly, looking, dropping their heads, stretching muzzles towards us. Murmuring gently there they lingered awhile. Then as suddenly as they had come, they turned and tails high cantered back to the spring grass. All but for one. Delilah's pair-bond – the gelding who had been her special friend – who used to move in unison with her as they grazed, or stand with her, nose to tail, swatting flies when the sun was high. He stayed for maybe 20 minutes. Waiting and watching. I wondered was he there for her or perhaps even for me. Eventually he, too, turned and walked slowly back to the rest of the herd.

I had never seen anything like it before. Usually, the horses grazed together in small groups of two or four. There were literally acres for them to roam around. They seldom came up to the gates at the farmyard, particularly in the height of spring when the grass was pushing through – they mostly stayed out at the furthermost edge of the farm, away from the yard.

Why did they come? And why then? Was it a coincidence? I didn't think so. Was it possible that they had sensed her falling somehow across the acres? Many years later, I would understand this parting gift of knowledge from Delilah: that horses communicate with each other, instantly, silently, in the moment, and across distance; that their language, and their most powerful sense, are of spirit and energy, not of sound or sight; that they converse with us too, if we can only learn how to listen and to speak with our hearts.

### *Presence brings peace*

Sitting with Delilah in the hours before her death, I also learned how to stay with the joy of her living, alongside the pain of what was to come. I lived each moment as if it were the only one, with yesterday and tomorrow suspended, and with my cares and worries related to both faded away, I existed, fully, vitally, for what was 'right now'.

I learned that when we can be absolutely present like this, our mind, body and spirit become integrated and we are fully conscious, energised, peaceful, alive, at one with the true essence of what it is to be ourselves. In that moment, we can relate with compassion to those around us and to ourselves. It is when what we have satisfies us, and when what we don't have doesn't matter. When we can find love within ourselves and don't depend on it from without. It is then that we are at peace. It is in this moment of completeness and presence that we can glimpse, and be, the human being that we are meant to be.

This is where Delilah took me, and where I would see other horses take my clients many years later.

## 4

## *Presence and Connecting with the Self*

Sitting in a circle on the hay bales in the barn as we did the round of introductions at the start of this two-day programme, George looked out of place. An entrepreneur in the advertising industry, his fashionable attire was suitable for a chilly day in Soho but in rural Wiltshire it would provide little protection from the elements. Shiny brogues, an immaculate black leather jacket with a petrol-blue cashmere scarf which coordinated perfectly with his extravagantly rimmed spectacles. Our introductory activity involved everyone selecting a photograph of a horse from a range of images on coloured cards. George chose one of a solitary, exquisitely beautiful, black horse standing in a meadow, head high and showing signs of being highly alert, on the lookout, its coat shining in the sunlight.

'I was drawn to its power, beauty, boldness,' he shared. 'Equally, I would be quite frightened of this horse if I met it in a field. I hope yours are smaller.' He chuckled nervously. 'I guess it reflects how I see myself as a leader because to win contracts I need to be as attractive to my clients as this picture was to me. It's such a competitive market. I also need to run the show with the team I lead. They need to look up to me like I do to this horse. You know, respect me.'

I thanked him; we finished the round of introductions and went out to work with the horses. George noticed that one of the herd was a hefty, almost black, horse and immediately asked if he could work with her. Her name was Autumn. The first stage of the process was simply for him to 'meet' the horse, to build trust with her such that, eventually, she would allow him to halter and groom her. But every time he got within eight feet of the horse, she moved away – not quickly, but enough to keep him at several arms' length. He turned and looked at me, shrugging his shoulders and lifting his palms to the sky in frustration.

'What's happening, George?' I asked.

'Well, the horse keeps leaving! I don't have a hope in hell of getting close.'

'And is there anything about what is happening which feels familiar?' I asked, causing him to fall silent for a moment in reflection.

'Well, interesting that you ask. I've been having a few problems in the past year or so with a couple of people in my team. They don't ever seem to do what I want them to do, in the way that I want. I always seem to be criticising them, which isn't doing anything for our relationship or their motivation. Or mine to be honest. I'm beginning to dread going to work in the morning, with the likely conflict I'll get. I've never felt like that about my business before. The other thing that occurs to me is that we have lost a couple of big clients recently, too, which has made me worried about where we are going wrong with those relationships. The really worrying thing is the news came right out of the blue, that they had switched agents. Usually, you'd get a whiff of it beforehand. Things feel like they are drifting away from me, a bit like the horse is.'

While he spoke, the horse carried on grazing, with an eye on him at all times. In the next paddock, others had succeeded in building rapport with their horses while he was still at first base.

'Thank you for sharing that, George. Would you like to try again with her? See what you need to change to help her feel more confident around you. Be curious about it.'

But the same pattern continued, and as his frustration grew, he became cross. So the mare put more and more distance between him and her. He turned and looked at me, furrowing his brow and dropping his arms in a slap onto the side of his thighs in exasperation.

'How are you doing?' I asked gently.

'This horse doesn't want to connect. I don't know what's wrong with her. All the others seem OK with doing the task with everyone else. Has she done this before?' His voice had a sharpness to it, the implication clearly that this lack of success was down to the horse or her level of experience. Or perhaps even mine.

I let his question drift away in the air. It didn't need a response. 'I am curious about how connected *you* feel right now?'

'I don't know what you mean,' he said blankly.

My question had been too oblique. 'I was wondering how connected you feel – you know, with yourself and with the surroundings here?'

He reflected, and frowning, replied, 'I still don't know what you mean.'

'OK,' I said, 'are you up for a little experiment? I will try to show you if that's OK?'

'Yeah, sure.' He didn't sound convinced but followed my instructions nonetheless as I asked him to close his eyes, feel his feet on the ground, to notice his breath as it entered and left his lungs and to imagine breathing any tension out of his muscles and into the fresh light breeze. Then, to hear the sounds all around us, the distant voices of the others in the group, the birdsong, the rustle of the breeze in the trees. We continued with our standing meditation for several minutes, maybe more; I noticed his breath was slowing and deepening, and the muscles in his face and fists were relaxing.

### *Connection through presence*

Without warning, the dark, shining horse lifted her head
from the grass and looked at him directly. Her ears and eyes
were on him. Her feet then followed, walking purposefully
towards him. His eyes were still closed, and so that she didn't
startle him, I said in the softest voice I could, 'George, the
horse is coming towards you. I am here and will keep you
safe; you can keep your eyes closed or open them.'

He chose to keep his eyes closed, and Autumn stopped a
neck's length from him, stretching out to sniff his hands.
Then she took a step nearer and placed her brow gently
against his chest. He opened his eyes and the moistness in
his eyes betrayed the depth of the emotion he felt.

'I can't believe that happened,' he said. 'That is
incredible. Now I know what you mean by connected with
myself. I don't think I can ever remember noticing so much,
or feeling so ... well *here* ... I suppose.'

I invited George to spend a few moments with Autumn –
further words were unnecessary. He had understood what he
needed to do in order to improve all his relationships, his
understanding of other people and also of himself. How to
become present. To be in the moment. To fully inhabit his
physical body. His cynicism was gone, and his need to blame
the horse (or me, or his team back at work) when things
didn't go as he wished. Instead, he knew he had to take
responsibility for the way in which he responded to others
and to the situations in which he found himself.

During the course of the next two days he continued to
open up, slow down and relax. Many of the horses seemed
to gravitate towards him and were both trusting and
respectful. We laughed that this was what he wanted from

both his team and his clients. On the second afternoon it was Autumn who thrilled him by weaving around the paddock glued to his shoulder without the aid of a halter or lead rope. When finally she came to rest at his side, she dozed peacefully while he stroked her neck.

Autumn had helped George to understand how much he had to gain from 'being' rather than 'doing'. He appreciated that the issues he was having with his team and clients stemmed from his own detachment and that he could improve this simply by being present. This beautiful near-black horse had taught him that by connecting with himself, in the moment, he could connect effortlessly with those around him.

### *The consciousness of good relationship*

It wasn't that George was neglectful of his relationships in his personal and professional life. He actually spent a lot of time and energy *thinking* about them. But he had simply forgotten how to 'be'.

It mattered not why this had happened, I was unaware of the cause as he probably was too. It could have been the pressure of his work, life experiences such as illness, bereavement or relationship breakdown, or a trauma experienced much earlier in his life, which caused him to disappear out of sight of himself. Now, with this horse, in this moment he had experienced what it felt like simply to exist, as himself, with full consciousness, in relationship with another. And after being reminded what it was like, he would be able to find his way back there when he needed to.

I wondered whether George had even created his time-starved, stressful lifestyle, like I did once, as a way of avoiding something he didn't want to face: strong emotions, loneliness, or difficult conversations he needed to tackle.

Perhaps while he was busy living in his mind rather than in his emotional body, unhappiness was more bearable.

To take a step into the moment, in touch with his true feelings as well as in conscious relationship with the people around him, I knew George had needed fortitude. And as he left at the end of that programme I hoped that this would stay with him and that he would be able to continue to embrace presence and reap the other rewards which it could bring.

George discovered that horses don't respond to people when they are caught up with the noisy mental process in their head and indeed that humans are the same. Yet when he was able to connect consciously with the felt sense of being in the moment this in turn would quiet his mind, alleviate his need to worry about what might and might not happen and clear the way for open communication.

It would not be easy, but finding presence was a skill which George could develop which in time would become a habit and later a way of being. Then it would help him to really change his life. I hoped that the memory which he had of standing with Autumn on that first day of his programme in Wiltshire would be the guiding light he needed.

## 5

# Gemma: Tragedy and Loss of Self

## Cambridgeshire, 1999

Several months after losing Delilah I was married and we moved to Cambridgeshire due to my husband's work. But not before I had sought out a new horse to go with me. I decided I would buy one younger than Delilah so we would not be parted so soon. I found Gemma. She reminded me of Carabella – strong and muscular with a dark brown coat and black mane with a white star on her forehead. Solid in stature and it seemed in personality. She loved to ride out around the lanes and byways. She was a horse who would look after me.

When we moved south I secured a senior role with a forward-thinking global company based locally. I couldn't believe my luck.

In my personal life things did not go so well. The older, charismatic man I had fallen for turned into something quite different once the vows were made. The realisation that my choice of partner had been based on many misguided assumptions and a pressing desire to have a family of my own began chipping away at my self-esteem, as did his controlling behaviour.

After three years, I was barely coping with the anxiety provoked by my life at home. It was a miserable way to live. One Sunday afternoon in September, I asked for some time alone. We walked and talked in a nearby country park, hands in pockets and gazing at the ground as it passed under our feet. It was not the first time I had tried to reason with him, but I told him that it would be the last. That if things didn't change, I would be gone.

The next morning the phone went as I was pouring milk onto my cereal at the breakfast bar. My husband was upstairs packing his bag for the week. He had been promoted again and was working away from Monday to Friday. It was unusual that anyone should call so early. It was the girlfriend of my husband's eldest son who had recently graduated with a Master's degree. He had gone missing, did we know where he was she asked. They had argued bitterly, he had stormed out and had not returned.

The next two days became a fretful waiting game. On the Tuesday night, we had received no news, and my husband decided to drive south for an important meeting he had the following day. Sitting by the phone was no use to anyone. After he left I settled on the sofa with Holly and Milo, our two Jack Russells. His two other sons were out, so the house was peaceful. I would have an early night, try to get some sleep. I had been alone for about an hour when there was a knock at the front door. The dogs ran barking into the hall as I made my way to answer. I peered through the peephole into the dark night. The shiny numbers on a policeman's jacket were all I could see.

I felt sick; I knew what this could mean.

The policeman came in, checked my name, and then asked if I was alone and if anyone could come to be with me. There wasn't, I said. So he told me as carefully as he could that my stepson's body had been found, on Eastbourne beach. He had drowned. The policeman wouldn't sit down. I wondered if he had done this before; he was uncomfortable.

'I am so sorry,' he said. 'Can I do anything to help you? Perhaps call your husband? Or send a police car to get him?'

'No, no, I think it is better coming from me,' I said.

'Well, if you're sure madam. We will be in touch again tomorrow to take your statements and that kind of thing. There will need to be an investigation.'

And with that I was left, icy and alone with the dreadful knowledge that this beautiful young man was dead. He was the gentle one in the family, my ally in the testosterone-fuelled, volatile household.

Now, the quality of my marriage and my personal happiness were of no consequence whatsoever. I knew that what happened next was out of my control and normality would elude me for a long time. I was deeply terrified.

When tragedy falls, sometimes this helps pull people together. To share love and kindness and find forgiveness. This was not the case for us. We buckled under the weight of our grief and the family imploded.

Fifteen months after the event, I was broken and was sure that I had no other option than to leave. Even with the counselling I had been having I simply couldn't take it anymore. It had become a matter of survival.

One of my friends had a granny flat adjacent to her house; her mother had passed away, and she offered it to me for a few months. It was also where I kept Gemma in the stables at the back. It would be ideal. I called the office to say I wouldn't be at work, then called my mum, Kate, my sister-in-law and a friend. They came, we loaded up all our cars, and I was gone. It took a couple of hours.

Finally alone and safe with my dogs in the silence of my rented accommodation, I collapsed onto the sofa and curled into a ball, shuddering in desperation. I felt like there was nothing left of me. Nothing at all. The ordeal had consumed everything that I had.

### The self disintegrates

The night that the policeman called, I became three people. There was the woman who stayed at the centre of the unfolding nightmare. Who dug deep to offer love, compassion and understanding in spite of her own shock, grief and unhappiness. The bride, once full of hope, who became smaller over the months, emptier and more desperate as each day passed. Then there was the strident and capable businesswoman, in her tailored suit and painted smile. This woman was brave, in control, competent and determined. The façade rarely weakened and was reinforced by her ability to focus on the job in hand, to find fun with her colleagues and keep very, very busy.

These two women, the wife and the professional, were not alone. They were observed silently by a girl of around fifteen years of age who looked on in horror. This was the girl who had come home one day from school to find that her father had left and that her mother was in pieces, as well as all the crockery which had been hurled in anger across the floor. For this girl, it was as if the years had not passed. She was still there with her school bag in her hand, watching as her world collapsed. Hoping that her life would return to normal. This time, though, she did not know if it ever would.

### Moments of integration

But sometimes, the three parts of me were able to take each other's hands with a firm but comfortable grip and walk side by side. The girl with hope and the businesswoman with strength put their arms around their suffering sister. The three became one again. Became me again. These were the times I spent riding Gemma.

Somehow, when I was astride her strong back, I was calm

and temporarily free from anguish. It was as if she rocked me as she walked. Soothed, I could absorb myself in nature, hear the birdsong, wonder at the vibrant palette of colour amongst the autumnal or spring hedgerows, fill my lungs with the fragrance of life itself. I became present, one person in one body, my nerves at rest.

Gemma looked after me – I knew that. She was steady, dependable, self-assured. Always willing to go, and always willing to slow, as I asked. We would go for miles in harmonious companionship. Those rides with her, and the lengthy walks with Holly and Milo my two youthful Jack Russells were what kept me sane.

Later on, when I understood the sensitivity and complexity of horses, only then I comprehended how strong and forgiving this horse had been to tolerate my emotional distress during this, one of the darkest periods of my life.

Yet often, when I was not in the saddle, Gemma would look at me and pin her ears back flat against her head. 'Stay away from me!' they warned. If I ignored her clear message, she would aim a hind foot, always accurately, bruising my flesh but not breaking my limbs. On those days, I learned to simply leave her in the paddock. I dared not go near her.

### *A friend lost*

A year after I left my husband, Gemma became lame. She had sustained a serious pelvic injury when I first bought her, perhaps falling in her field or stable. After 6 months rest and rehabilitation she had recovered well, and although would never make a competition horse she had been untroubled by the injury since. But now it was deteriorating again, quickly. The vet ordered X-rays and a bone scan, which only confirmed the bad news. There was not much that could be done.

I planned that, like Delilah, she would stay retired for as long as possible, at pasture, and I would make the most of the time we had left together. But, unlike Delilah, she did not come to me for comfort, and I could not share the treasured times as we had together. She did not like to be around me. Who could blame her? I was an emotional mess, tense and anxious. She was also in pain. So we became distant, disjointed. If only I had understood then how to listen to her, how to let her help me.

Then there were other medical complications, and the vet and I both felt it was time to call it a day. I said goodbye but this time didn't have it in me to see her go. Afterwards I felt that I had let her down.

A few months after I lost Gemma, the professional façade which I had so carefully constructed, the part of me that was still functioning, was also to take a battering. My job was made redundant. I had relied on it for more than a salary. It gave me the part of myself that was still relatively reliable. It gave me my sense of who I thought I was. The status that came with my position and the recognition I received was what helped me to feel valuable, worthy. Now all that, too, was gone.

## 6

## *You Can't Fool a Horse*

I know now that I failed my second horse, Gemma, when I attributed her sometimes aggressive behaviour to her hormonal cycle. Later, when I learned how sensitive horses are to every nuance of our emotions, intentions and authenticity, I grasped that when she lashed out it was me she was responding to. I could pretend to the world that I was 'fine' – the successful optimistic woman who could cope with anything – but I couldn't fool Gemma. She was not taken in for one minute by my façade. The saying goes, you can fool some people all of the time, or all people some of the time. But you can never fool a horse, any of the time.

Horses need to know that what they see on the outside of a person matches what is on the inside. That makes them feel safe. And they notice immediately, and tell you, if it doesn't. Gemma was direct and she usually chose to communicate with her hooves. She didn't care about hurting me or my feelings. Horses don't. They are honesty in its purest form. If you are pretending in any way, as I was, they let you know. Most will be more gentle with how they communicate their message – using perhaps a swish of the tail or nudge with the shoulder or movement of the ears – but it will be evident nonetheless if you know what to look for.

Equally, when you find a way of integrating the splinters of your self, horses notice instantly and give you immediate positive reinforcement. They shine a light into your soul, see what goes unnoticed to the rest of the world, and bring it to your awareness. If you let them show you, you can get to discover your *true* self, a self that you might like more than you thought you would. I'd learn later how to let my horses guide me and also my clients in this way, and that if I listened to what they had to say it could change everything.

### *Personal power and authenticity*

Bob came to work with me to develop his leadership skills. As he introduced himself, I noticed that he tended to avoid eye contact, looking downward, and he hesitated before speaking.

'I think I am respected for my technical skills – my team likes me too. What is really frustrating me though is that they are always missing deadlines and making stupid mistakes. My boss then comes down on me like a ton of bricks. I've tried and tried again but can't seem to motivate them to really stretch themselves to achieve the high standards they need to. To be better at solving problems themselves and delivering top-class solutions.'

I then asked him how he would describe himself as a leader:

'I like to be quite formal, you know, keep a distinction between how I am at home and how I am at work. People respect you for that. Especially since I was promoted some years ago. You have to keep your distance a bit.'

I thanked Bob, and when the rest of the group had finished their introductions we went to begin the real work of the day – with the herd. It came to Bob's turn to meet the horses. He stepped away from the fence rubbing his hands together and then burying them deep into his pockets. The horses glanced at him with indifference as he approached then continued determinedly with their feasting. He tried all sorts of things to get their attention. But effectively it was as if, for them, he wasn't there.

We explored various ideas that he could experiment with to improve his physical presence and impact. But the horses still ignored him. I then asked him what his passion was. He looked a bit surprised at such a question:

'What do you mean?'

'What gets your blood running through your veins? What makes you buzz? What would you find most difficult to give up in life? What would you like most to share with your kids when they grow up and you spend time together?'

'Oh, that's easy.' He beamed. 'Mountain biking.'

'OK, so tell me about your best ever mountain biking experience.' And as he talked about his last biking trip to the French Alps, taking the ski lift up the mountain and racing down, the exhilaration of it, the risk, the views, the achievement of getting down in one piece, his whole being lit up. He became taller, more energised, more present. He literally transformed before my eyes.

'Wow, that sounds wonderful. With that image in your mind, go and ask the horse you'd like to get to know, to go with you. Take the halter and rope. We often don't use them, so the horses can vote with their feet. But in this case I think it would be helpful.'

Bob looked concerned. 'I don't want to force her though. That doesn't seem fair.'

'First of all, with the images of your mountain adventure in your mind, you will need to win the horse's trust in order that she accepts the equipment. Fear not, if you don't do so she won't allow you to put it on her. And once it's on, if you communicate with her respectfully and clearly, like we practised earlier, the horse will come willingly.'

Bob smiled. 'Right, I see … and if I try to force her she won't come anyway, is that it?'

'You got it! Think of the rope like a telephone line, not a

control device. It is a communication tool they are used to. Now go and take her biking.'

Bob walked across to one of the mares, Holly, who was still grazing. As he extended the back of his hand in greeting she sniffed it and didn't drop her nose again into the grass. He stroked and scratched her on the shoulder and her neck bent in a graceful arc towards his hip. It looked a gentle gesture. The mare waited patiently while he worked out how to slip the halter up onto her nose, passing the strap behind her ears and securing it with the buckle lying flat against her left-hand cheek. Respectfully he invited Holly to walk with him. She took one step, then two and then her pace quickened alongside his. They had nearly completed an entire lap of the field when she broke into a trot, matching his pace. He beamed.

Bob had confused having healthy boundaries between his professional and personal worlds with creating an alternative version of himself who went to work. He had done it in an attempt to create 'distance' between himself and those who reported to him, believing that they would respect him more and therefore perform better in their jobs. Instead he became a one-dimensional figure whom they did not find convincing.

When Bob left his true self at the office entrance, he also left behind his passion, his energy, his vibrancy. He became bland and colourless. He learned with Holly that all he had to do to inspire and motivate his team was to stay connected with what was important to his soul.

Constructing and maintaining a façade as Bob did, and as I had done for most of my professional career, takes effort whether you do it consciously or unconsciously. While you put energy into who you are not, you can't put it into who you are. You can't ever explore your true potential while you underinvest in your real, essential self.

## 7

# *After Gemma*

## *Cambridgeshire, 2001*

### *Back to school*

Still building strength after my divorce and with a new
mortgage to service, when my job disappeared I accepted a
different position with the same company instead of taking
redundancy. Although giving me financial security for a
little longer, the role was effectively a significant demotion
which didn't suit my natural abilities. In spite of my
colleagues who were kind, caring and compassionate, I soon
found, for the first time in my life, that I was struggling to
get myself to the office on time in the mornings. This lack of
motivation was debilitating and I wished I could shake it off.
I missed having a horse, too, and the feeling of wellbeing it
brought.

Maybe I had come to the end of the road in my corporate
career? The need to please others and fit in with their
priorities and values was wearing thin and I yearned to find
a way of getting back to doing what I loved: helping people
to fulfil their potential. And I had to do it in a way which
didn't involve signing up to another employment contract. I
needed an alternative career. After some months' reflection
and research, I signed up to train as a psychotherapist.

As part of the training, I was told that I would have to
undertake psychotherapy myself. I muttered that I didn't

need it, there was nothing wrong with me, but as it was a compulsory part of the training I conceded under protest. I was still putting on a brave face to fool the world and also myself in the process. In reality, I was in tatters. Gemma had seen that but I was still in denial.

The first day of the course came. The room we met in wasn't what I had expected. The walls were a pale shade of pinkish white, and at the patio doors, delicate curtains billowed in the breeze. Outside, the garden was lined with crazy colourful borders boasting their autumnal festival of dahlias, lupins and late roses. Nine of us sat cross-legged in a circle around the edge of the room on cushions and mattresses. Our teacher also sat on the floor, dressed elegantly in metres of natural fabric.

There was much talk of 'energy', 'process' and 'embodiment', words which drifted past my comprehension. On the second weekend, I was asked by our trainer to share how my process was moving within me. I didn't have a clue what she meant.

I soon would. This was not a programme of study where I would simply turn up two weekends a month for four years and acquire new skills and a shiny certificate. It was like an emotional laundry where all of us brought our dirty washing. Our respective traumas and struggles were unpacked, thrown into the machine together, washed, spun, dried and aired. Eventually we would be able to fold our issues neatly away again.

This was the place where, amongst friends and fellow students, it was possible to unravel in safety and I didn't need to be brave any more. Here there was no place for façade and we listened patiently and lovingly to each other's sorrows, hopes and fears. I learned to sit silently and compassionately alongside and within pain and trauma – both my own and others' – and allow the magnitude of my formative experiences to emerge. In this place, the three fragmented versions of me found a voice and another way of becoming one, as they had astride Gemma's gracious back.

## *Our bodies speak*

The psychotherapy school I attended offered training in a modality called Body Psychotherapy. This doesn't only involve *talking* about what troubles you. It assumes a profound connection between mind, body and spirit, and that our emotional experience lives in the very tissue of our physical form. I learned that what we feel in the moment, and have felt during our lifetime, affects our muscle tone and tension, our breathing and our posture and that this in turn defines the kind of energy we radiate, and therefore attract. What I discovered within this nurturing programme of study would, in time, help me unlock the incredible power of horses as healers and teachers.

If the hypothesis of my training was true, no wonder that for a horse, who can sense a fly landing on her back and communicate non-verbally with the herd over great distances, our emotions are utterly transparent.

This new knowledge and understanding came at the right time. Soon the next horse to come into my life would show me how little I knew about myself.

## 8

## *Winston: Loss Unfolding*

**Cambridgeshire 2001**

The vibrant energy and mischievous eye of this patchwork horse captivated me from the first moment I saw him on that freezing November day.

I had decided after Gemma that I would not get another horse so that I could focus on my psychotherapy studies which were intensive – taking up two weekends out of four during term time. Yet as autumn came and the flush of vibrant colours spread through the hedgerows and those first crisp mornings heralded the approach of winter, I became aware that without a horse my life felt empty. I liked to ride and missed that, but it was the very presence of a horse, and the peacefulness I felt when I was with them which I longed for. I could purge my lungs of the stale office air by spending a couple of hours outdoors, close to nature, mucking out the stable or grooming.

So when a friend called me to say that she knew of a lovely gelding coming up for sale locally, I could not resist going to see him. That was how I met Winston. I rode him a few times; we liked each other. I got the vet out to check him, he passed, and so several days later, I bought him. He was going to be exactly what I needed to relax and to help get me through my psychotherapy course. Or so I thought …

### *My mother decides*

'How did you get on then?' I asked chirpily. Mum had unusually called me at work. I knew she would want to share the results of her tests with me as soon as possible so I wasn't surprised. It was March. She had been having minor gastric problems, an ulcer was suspected and a gastroscopy arranged. It seemed uncomplicated.

There was an uncomfortable pause where I had expected a cheery update. Something was wrong.

'Sweetheart, I'm so sorry. The doctor told me that I have stomach cancer. They say it's early days and with some minor surgery and radiotherapy I should be OK. I'll know more after the MRI scan next week. Try not to worry.'

I couldn't believe it. She was well, apart from the digestive grumblings she'd had. I sat down, struggling to take in the news.

We nervously awaited the scan a week later and hoped for surgery and a swift conclusion. But the cancer had already spread. She was given six months, maybe eighteen, if the chemotherapy worked.

'No,' she said firmly when I travelled up to see her the following weekend. 'I am NOT having any chemo, and please don't ask me to. I've discussed it with Lorenz and told him my decision. If I'm going to die soon, I want to enjoy the time I have left on the planet, not be ill all the time. I have got too much to do, to be in and out of hospital.'

So, that was that. She wouldn't be convinced, and we quickly gave up trying. She had made her mind up.

So she and her second husband Lorenz sat down and planned all the places they wanted to visit or revisit in their beloved mobile home, which had taken them on so many adventures the length and breadth of Europe and in particular, Spain. Now, Mum would not be covered under medical insurance to travel outside the UK. But there was still enough in our own country that they wanted to experience. Every trip they took, I would receive one or two postcards that I would treasure – always with a few loving and cheery lines hastily written. How these times must have been for them I cannot imagine, precious moments tinged so deeply with dread of what was to come.

## *My horse doesn't deserve a bullet*

Until this point Winston and I had been getting on well. But as my emotional state deteriorated in parallel to my mother's health, his behaviour when ridden changed and became increasingly extreme. Soon, he would rear if I as much as put a foot in the stirrup. Unsurprisingly, I gave up the idea of riding him at all. I was too frightened.

But around the stable yard, he soon became equally dangerous – he'd push me around, barge me out of the way and run me over. I had been lucky with Delilah and Gemma – they had both been willing to look after me. But Winston was different; he was younger and a more dominant, demanding horse. I had run out of knowledge and didn't know what to do about him. Soon, what was meant to be my emotional panacea had turned into my nightmare. When I most needed relief he was at his most explosive. I became terrified of him.

Advice from the unsympathetic equestrian professionals I consulted progressed from, 'He's being naughty!' to 'Man up and sort him out! Show him who's boss!' to finally, 'He needs a bullet; he's dangerous!'

But I sensed that it wasn't his fault. Eventually, I found someone who said she would come and help me with Winston – a newly qualified riding teacher who said she had a sticky bottom, and he didn't worry her at all. I told her all about how bad he had been. She nodded, tacked him up, strapped on her hat and got on. He didn't bat an eyelid. She rode him out of the stable yard and returned smiling an hour later. That was all the proof I needed. My horse wasn't crazy, evil, or deserving of the slaughterhouse. I knew with certainty his behaviour was about me. I just didn't know what to do about it. And I had too much to deal with to even make a start in finding out.

## 9

## *Mum: Making up Lost Time*

### *Our parents' pedestals*

My relationship with my mother had foundered in my twenties as I came to understand that she had driven a wedge between me and my father when they divorced. In spite of her happiness with Lorenz, with whom she went on to have nearly 25 years of loving union, she had never been able to forgive my dad or let me and my brothers forget how he had betrayed her. Her bitterness ran deep, and she would lay the guilt on us whenever we visited or spoke of him, even once we reached adulthood.

As a teenager, I had accepted my mother's version of what kind of man my father was: weak, cruel, unfaithful, deceitful. He was not the hero I had always worshipped and hadn't loved any of us enough to stay. My innocent heart was splintered into a million pieces and with it my trust of him.

In womanhood, an increasingly independent eye changed my perspective. I noticed how Mum liked to control those around her and how her vivid, powerful energy made it difficult for a more introverted person, a husband, or a daughter, to be themselves. Her bright light was so strong that mine would flicker and die in her orbit. I saw why I had been a quiet, compliant child, and why my father, a gentle and passive man, might have fallen in love with someone else, who allowed him to shine.

I had been wrong to judge my father as my mother had.

Years of relationship and potentially happy times had been needlessly lost. I forgave him for leaving and eventually was even able to tell him that. But finding pardon for my mother for making my child-self hate him so much – that was harder.

With my shifting view on their break-up, the way in which my mother still tried to manipulate me was more evident and I began to assert myself. She would flounce out of the room, or slam the phone down. Eventually, I would cave in and apologise. I was still the obedient child who needed her approval. She would be frosty at first, and then over a few weeks, normality would return. That was the pattern.

Then there was a rupture from which I thought we might never recover. I disagreed with her over a family matter, and the savagery of her verbal assault left me stunned. This time, it was me who put the phone down and I vowed that it would not be me, either, who would pick it up first. It was she who owed me an apology.

We did not speak for months. Eventually, she called me although did not mention our argument. We pretended it never happened; it was too hard for me to ask her why she had said what she did. But things were never really the same. What had been spoken could not be withdrawn and I always held something of myself back after that time. The pedestal I had placed her on was as shattered as my father's had been those years earlier.

### *An everyday love*

Notwithstanding these difficulties, I had continued to love her as a daughter does. But now she was ill, I knew we had some ground to make up – and quickly. We didn't do much out of the ordinary – going into Liverpool city centre shopping, cooking meals together, perhaps exchanging a manicure. Our conversation was mostly mundane, this and that, my work, my course, my love life. In spite of the gravity of her situation there was mostly laughter; her spirit was as indomitable as ever. She was a woman who liked to have fun. She didn't want to talk about her illness, or about dying. Often we would reminisce about happy times and shared memories.

One evening, we were recalling the time that she and Lorenz had come to visit me as a student in France. I was spending the third year of my degree at the University of Pau, near the Pyrenees. On the first day of their visit, we had set off to drive into the mountains for a day out. The car had broken down, and we ended up on the forecourt of a rural garage while we waited for the mechanic to finish his lunch. If it wasn't bad enough to eat our packed lunch amongst the pungent petroleum vapours, the roadside picnic table and matching stools were in the shape of large red toadstools with white spots. As each French car passed, the disbelieving occupants wrinkled their faces into a scornful pout. These English – they come to this outstanding landscape and look where they choose to take their picnic!

'We must have looked like large gnomes!' Mum hooted. 'And the look on their faces, they must have thought we were crazy. And then next day, the damn car broke down again! And you had to go for help on that slurry-covered tractor with the old pig farmer.'

We had told every detail of that story, many times, over many years, but the delight was in sharing in it again while we could.

'Happy days,' I said. I had intended the comment cheerfully, but my words were swallowed by a wistful, painfully poignant silence.

'There will be many more darling, you know that, don't you? You will have a lot more happy days to come. There are better times ahead. When … when …' her voice trailed away. 'When … this … is all over.'

I put my arms around her and laid my cheek on her shoulder.

'I'm so proud of you Mum; how courageous you are, dealing with all this. You are so brave.'

'No, I'm not darling,' she said firmly but kindly. 'I'm not brave at all. If I had been, I would not have behaved as I did to your father all those years ago. I know I spoiled things for you. And I want to say I am sorry. It was wrong of me. I should not have turned you all against him like I did. I hope you can forgive me.'

Her words left me speechless. I had wanted to hear them for so many years; now I could say or do nothing other than squeeze her hand in mine. I told her that of course I had forgiven her but a quiet voice inside asked if really I had.

Leaving her at the end of those visits was always the hardest part. We would stand in their hallway, she cradling me in her arms. There were no words. Salty eyes scrunched closed, and my nose running onto her shoulder like a small child, I'd desperately try to imprint the feel and scent of her in my memory. I knew that one day, soon, it would be the last time we would say goodbye. But I never guessed how our last embrace would be.

As Christmas drew closer and her health petered away, my life was on hold and full of pain. I became conscious that I was now waiting for her to die. For the terminally ill and their loved ones, there are 10,000 deaths, all but one of them are imagined and no less painful. I didn't want to lose her, but I also knew I had to before things could get any better. This poisonous paradox made me ashamed of my selfish spirit and lay silently like a toxic fog in the harrowing silences between us when we could pretend no more.

## *The last embrace*

After several false alarms Mum was admitted to the hospice for what would be the last time. I dropped everything again and made the drive up to Liverpool. I was too late to see her while conscious, to say precious last words. But there had been so many already, there was little left unsaid. She was on a morphine pump when I arrived. It couldn't be long now.

That night, none of us wanted to leave her bedside, but it was getting late, and the nurse advised it could be a couple of days yet. Lorenz looked exhausted as was I. He was 83 years old and I was worried about him. So we all went to get some sleep.

I was staying with Lorenz at their house. I was in Mum's bed – she and Lorenz had separate rooms. It felt strange to be there, but it was also comforting to be surrounded by her things. Surprisingly, I fell instantly asleep as my head hit the pillow.

It was dark when I awoke at 4am and I was unsure what had roused me so abruptly. As I slowly pulled myself out of my numbing sleep, I realised that I could sense Mum in the room. My conscious self sought explanation, perhaps it was her scent which lingered on her clothes and played tricks with me. I opened my eyes and reached further for wakefulness. No, this wasn't merely a memory invoked, she *was* actually there. I could feel her in the room with me. In the darkness, her presence, the one that soothed all ills, was unmistakable. She was all around me, enfolding me in her arms and bathing me in her warm, tender and ferocious love. I pushed myself up off the pillows, confused and searching to make sense of what was happening in the pitch black of the night. What was going on? Was I really still asleep, and having a waking dream about her? Then the phone rang.

It was the night sister at the hospice. She softly broke the news that a few moments earlier Mum had passed away. 'Oh, my God,' I murmured. 'She came to say goodbye.'

Could this be? Had her spirit come to embrace me one last time? Or had grief upset the clarity of my mind? I wasn't sure, but what I did know was that I would always have her with me.

## 10

## *Winston: Teaching me to Choose Courage*

After Mum's passing, things went from bad to worse with Winston. There were times when I would have given him away if someone had offered to take him but there was little chance of that. I'd clearly been naïve to assume that horses supplied solace on demand. Winston certainly did not – and why should he? I had little to offer him. Instead he tested me at every turn. But what I would learn from him would change my life.

### *Discovering the mind and body connection*

Apprehension was dominating my existence. Whenever I contemplated deviating from my safe daily routine the psychological and physical symptoms of panic would kick in: imagining catastrophes, obsessive checking of my house-leaving ritual (doors, windows, hob), sweating palms and shortness of breath. Going away for the weekend or on holiday, meeting new people, even walking the dogs at a different time or place could all trigger the same reality-bending response. Some days I could barely leave the house and when I did I was invariably late. I didn't tell anyone – I was a coper after all. This wasn't me. The accumulated experience of my marriage, the death of my stepson, divorce and watching my mother die had taken a significant toll on my way of being in the world. When I stepped out of my door I was putting on a smile, but inwardly I was churning and my world was getting smaller by the day.

Fortuitously, in the psychotherapy training room I was learning a range of approaches to anxiety management, mindfulness and grounding, including how to track and moderate the physical sensations which accompanied my emotional experiences. Lessons which probably saved me from the doctor's surgery. By being more aware of how my body reacted from one moment to the next, I could notice the particular patterning of muscular tension and constriction of my lungs which accompanied my psychosomatic cycle. If I could tune into these changes early enough and consciously soften my muscles and diaphragm I found that I could avoid being overwhelmed. Instead, my sadness or panic washed through me like a wave, leaving me peaceful and calm.

These were techniques which later I would use with my clients but for now they helped me to stabilise as I put them into practise on a regular basis. The heightened personal awareness which resulted made it then a natural progression to start paying attention to how my physical and emotional state affected my horse from one moment to the next.

When feelings of panic took hold of me, as my teeth clenched and my toes and fingers curled stiffly, Winston's own jaw would set, and he'd try to get away from me if he could. If he was tied up or enclosed in the stable with me, he'd nip or push me with his hefty shoulder. Yet once I learned to breathe my sorrows out and soften my muscles, his head would drop, his great rib cage would expand and he would let out a grateful sigh.

### Curious about my fear

As Winston's feedback helped me find my way back to a more consistent state of mind, it seemed possible that I might be able to conquer my most deep-seated fears and ride him again one day. I started keeping a journal to try and work out how I was going to do it. What surfaced was that trying to deny my powerful instinct for self-preservation in a rational way didn't work. The more I told myself 'I shouldn't' be afraid, the more rigid I became. So I decided to try and make a friend of my fear, it had served me well at times in my life. Could I be curious about what it had to tell me and then decide whether I still needed that advice to keep me safe? Then thank it for its care and invite it politely to leave my body with each outbreath I cultivated?

### *Winston responds*

As I interrogated my worries, their power diminished. Winston's behaviour became kinder around me although he was still clearly in charge. Then one evening he came to meet me at the gate which he had not done for some time.

'Hey buddy,' I extended the back of my hand towards him and he casually extended his long pink tongue in a languid lick across my skin. I reached my other hand into his wild, white mane and leant my face on his neck. My unanticipated catharsis left my eyes swollen and ribs aching. He stood nuzzling me gently. Where was the horse, now, who had scared me so much? As I allowed my emotions painful but authentic expression, it became clear that, actually, I hadn't been frightened of him at all. Not really. It was life alone, without a husband, without my mother, which darkened my horizon.

Later on, I reflected on this relational dance with Winston. I was beginning to grasp why he might have been behaving as he had. What he clearly liked was when I was being honest about how I felt whether it was sadness, excitement, anger, frustration. It was when I was suppressing feelings that he felt wary of me. He couldn't trust me when I

54

was pretending. And horses need trust. In its absence he needed to take charge or get me out of his space, or both. Conversely when I was true to how I felt and let my emotions flow, he knew what he was dealing with. He could rely on me, respect me, and help me.

### *Learning to let fear go*

I carried on building mastery of my erratic nervous system, being particularly mindful to be congruent when I was around Winston. Our mutual confidence and ability to relax together grew. Then one day, with the summer sun shining, and a light breeze fanning his opulent black and white tail, I felt peaceful, and so did he. I decided to put the saddle and bridle on him. It went well; he accepted both willingly. I hesitantly put my left foot in the stirrup. He still didn't move, so I swung my other leg over him. After sitting in the saddle for a few minutes, I checked my body, making sure that there was no panic creeping back in. There was, manifesting in a curling of my toes and clenching of my jaw.

Come on Pam you can do this, I reassured myself. Winnie, we can do this together. Keep breathing, keep the muscles soft, keep present, keep your faith. And so I gently asked Winston to walk on. He followed my suggestion, and we left the mounting block. I relaxed deep into the saddle, reins loose in one hand, the other stroking his solid neck. As he walked steadily and confidently along the bridle path, I gasped inwardly, 'We're doing it, we're actually doing it!'

The most wonderful thing was not that I was riding my horse again. Nor that I had rediscovered harmony with him. It was that finally I had succeeded in letting go of my fear. I had learned how to choose whether to be calm or whether to be afraid. I was learning how to make choices about how I responded to what had happened to me. Winston had taught me how to opt for courage, like my mother had in the face of her illness, rather than be a victim of my circumstance.

And all this turned on its head my perception of the nature of horses. They were not some passive panacea to salve the human soul. They were creatures of infinite complexity, capable of taking us to the core of our emotional experience. What I learned in these months with Winston would form the basis of the work I would later do with him, and other horses, to help people from all walks of life to embrace change and reach for the happy life they deserved.

## 11

## *Accepting the Need to Change*

Winston helped me to be honest with myself. He showed me when I was denying my emotional experience by putting on a brave face. This was when he felt the most unsafe with me. He also guided me to the understanding that he was not the real source of my anxiety, it was facing the world without my mother. In time I learned to take control of my panic button and calm my troubled mind. Winston then rewarded me with softness, playfulness, respect and trust. Some years later, he would help one of my clients in the same way.

### *In the grip of panic*

Anna was employed by a conference and events manager for a large multinational. She had worked her way up from the position of secretary/PA to the marketing director during the 16 years that she had worked for the company. Her passion was playing the piano, although she had not done so for a long time. Her busy job, looking after the home and her elderly parents seemed to take every minute.

In spite of being successful in her role, Anna had been having panic attacks when she attended important customer meetings or delivered presentations in front of a group. She had managed to cover her tracks but increasingly this was causing difficulty. She had finally discussed it with her manager who recommended that she seek help.

We worked with a number of techniques, both to help

develop Anna's confidence in the situations that she was finding difficult and to manage the nervousness that was arising. After several visits her condition was getting worse rather than better. Something wasn't right but I did not know what.

It was a blustery day in March with a cold easterly blowing and we were both clad in layers of warm clothing with only our faces exposed to the numbing chill. To date, Anna had worked with one of the mares, who had a soft, gentle presence. I was curious when this time she chose to work with Winston – my bossy horse. She looked intimidated and seemed to shrink under her rounded shoulders as she approached him.

After she had spent a little time observing Winston from a distance, Anna said she'd like to go and get him so she could groom him for a while. He willingly accepted the halter, but when she tried to move him he stood rooted. When she reached the end of the rope which had slipped slowly through her fingers she gave it a little tug, but he still didn't move. She returned to him, stroked his neck, and then asked him again to walk forwards. This time, he took a few steps but then again planted himself firmly on the spot.

This pattern continued for some while, the woman cajoling and imploring the horse each time he stopped. 'Come on Winnie, good boy, just one more step.' Her kindness and patience seemed endless, and not for a moment did she get frustrated. But each time he planted himself, her will diminished and her stature with it. Eventually she gave up, eyes cast downwards.

'What do you see, Anna, right now?' I asked.

'I see the ground. The muddy, hard ground.'

'And what would you like to see?'

She looked up. 'I'd like to see …' she paused. 'I'd like to see ... I don't know. I'd like to see something else. To *be* somewhere else. All I can see is the mess I am in. I don't even know what else there is.'

'So, if you look away from there,' I pointed at the spot in front of her feet, 'and choose somewhere different – where would that be, where would you choose?'

She looked up and waved an arm towards the horizon, beyond the willow tree at the edge of the paddock. 'Over there, way over there,' she said. 'As far as you can see, away into the horizon. Where it's less cold,' she laughed.

'OK, so look over there, towards the horizon. And don't look with only your eyes. Lift your chin and look with your whole body. Let your body follow your eyes.'

Anna lengthened her spine, her shoulders fell backwards, and she tilted her chin upwards.

'The horizon is higher than that, Anna, look further,' I urged. 'And now walk. And believe that Winston will follow you. Take him somewhere else. Take him where you want to go. And don't forget to breathe!'

She stepped forward, rigidly at first as she held this new, unnatural posture. But Winston took a step nonetheless. Surprised, she turned to face him.'

'Don't look back, Anna, keep going.'

She turned away, straightened up and walked. Again he followed, right by her side with a loop of slack in the rope. And so she strode, then marched, across the field, the stocky horse beside her. His ears were pricked and his interest piqued. As they walked together, Anna seemed to keep on getting taller.

'Go on,' I shouted through the bitter breeze. 'I know you want to run. Go for it!' And with that, she leapt forwards, the horse bouncing into a trot to keep up with her. They ran until she had to double over to catch her breath. Her smile almost broke her face in two. Winston was alert but calm, and happy to rest by her side.

Anna had flexed some new emotional and physical muscles and as her body had moved now the words, too, shifted. She spoke of living in a controlling domestic situation in which she felt vulnerable and worthless. There was no physical violence, but she was frightened of her husband's explosive temper, which erupted easily whenever she displeased him. It was clear that the panic that Anna was experiencing was less to do with her job than her relationship at home.

'I know I have to leave, I know I do, it's making me ill.' Her tone was fraught. 'To be honest staying seems more scary now than leaving. Yet leaving ... that's always seemed too daunting. But, if I can move half a ton of horse to my new horizon – then I guess I can move myself!'

It took a long time for Anna to prepare herself for change. It wasn't going to happen overnight. She engaged in regular counselling with a therapist closer to home and started taking piano lessons, which helped soothe her system and focus her in self-nurturing activity. She slowly built up a stronger sense of herself, so that she could be ready for a new life on her own. She let me know about a year later that she had moved into a flat by herself, and although it was hard, it was nowhere near as hard as her life had been before.

### The problem with being brave

Anna had become highly skilled at being brave. It was no longer a useful short term strategy for facing issues and getting on with her life. It had become her default setting by which she denied her needs and the reality of her predicament. This was affecting her health and her ability to envision a way out of her unhappiness. Continuing stoically as if all was in order allowed her to soldier on but without hope of changing anything. On the contrary it made it harder for her to move forwards because with it went the seductive proposition that 'everything is fine' which she had ended up believing herself.

### *Learn to love not knowing*

Apprehension about what her life would be like if she left her familiar world had been keeping Anna locked in a damaging relationship. Getting to know her fear intimately released her from its hold. She also understood, the day when she ran alongside Winston, that in reality she could never be certain about what was round the corner. But if she strode out towards the new nonetheless, she created the possibility of something good coming to her. She might find herself in previously uncharted territory without a map or rule book. But if she could become comfortable with *not knowing* what would happen, then uncertainty could become a place of promise.

## 12

### *Building Resilience*

For Anna, the first step to changing involved acknowledging that she needed to, and from there she learned to manage the disquiet which an uncertain future provoked. Building her emotional strength before she tackled the difficult decisions she had to make was also of utmost importance. Anna was able to remove herself from the situation which was so unhealthy for her. Sometimes though, that is not possible and all you can do is to support your well-being and change your relationship with the problem that you face.

Justine was part of a senior management team who came to work with me when their relationships became fractious. The organisation was in the midst of a period of prolonged change, and they had all been working hard. They had specifically asked for the programme to include content around building resilience and coping better under stress. As well as the pressure of work, Justine had also moved house recently, had teenagers doing exams, and her mother-in-law was seriously ill. So there was little respite for her, and her family members were all feeling the pain too. She shared that she hadn't slept a full night for months, was permanently exhausted and irritable, had piled on the pounds, and was drinking more wine than she knew she should to wind down in the evenings.

Justine had struggled to sit still during the initial introductions in the classroom, and later when she went to meet the horses, they reflected her vigilance. Whenever she approached them, they moved away. When she was walking with them and halted, they carried on going. Although she was physically stopping, inwardly everything was still racing and the horses tuned into this energy.

### *From anxiety to relaxation*

I started the afternoon with a short meditation in the field which involved developing conscious breath and muscle control whilst observing the herd. By learning to calm our minds and bodies in this way it is possible to short circuit our automatic stress response and build mental resilience.

I checked in with the team after the meditation to see how they all were, and what they wanted from the next session.

'I feel so chilled!' chimed Justine. 'All I want is to carry on feeling like this. It's brilliant! Can I go first?'

The group agreed and stood back. Returning to engage again with the horses, she sidled up alongside Beau, a large chestnut with a white blaze down his face who grazed several feet away. She matched the movement of his hefty hooves as he meandered, nibbling at the clover. Soon Beau stopped beside her. Finally I knew that Justine was beginning to slow down from the inside out.

'OK – I'm done now, Beau came! Success! And I'm still calm!' she said stepping away from the horse and dusting her hands off.

A wrinkling around Beau's lips and visible tension through his ribs suggested that he thought differently.

'Are you sure?' I said. 'Why don't you stay with him a little longer? I'm not sure he's ready for you to leave yet. See if you can breathe as slow and deeply as him. Watch his ribs, and match the movement as you were matching his footfall.'

Justine took her place beside Beau and for several moments slowed her breathing, watching the great ribs rise and fall softly. Then Beau reached skyward in the most comical yawn, stretching his tongue and lips to reveal rectangular teeth and pink gums. He shook his head blowing out several times through velvet nostrils. Now I knew that the job was done.

'Am I keeping you up?' Justine's eyes sparkled with childlike delight and the horse nuzzled her as if in reply.

'How are you now?' I asked.

'Oh, boy I feel great. I mean – really great! Really happy,' she said. 'Do you know, I had forgotten what it was like to laugh. I must do it more often. We must all do it more often.'

### *Healthy coping mechanism*

Six months later, I bumped into Justine at another programme. Her circumstances had not changed. But she had. Instead of accepting that the arduous demands placed on her would dictate the quality of her well-being, she had taken action to invest in it. She was going to yoga once a week, running when she could and drinking a lot less wine. She had more energy at home and the office, was sleeping well and was more effective at work.

Justine also shared with me that she was surprised to find that the calmer she got the more energised she became. She had confused relaxation with low energy, and living on adrenalin with being animated. By finding a new way of responding to her stressful family life she generated greater resources to deal with it as well as focus on her own leisure and self-care.

## 13

## *Coop: Chosen by a Horse*

### *Colorado, 2008*

The tyres hit gravel when we turned off the highway. It was 17 May 2008. I was arriving at a ranch high up in the mountains of the San Juan National Forest in Colorado where one of the world's best known natural horsemanship teachers ran a study centre. I was there for 6 weeks of intensive learning.

The car sent up a dust cloud as it crawled along the track up the hillside. Beyond the meadows where horses and cattle were roaming the majestic mountains rose, dense with dark green pine. An eagle circled slowly against the bright blue sky.

It had taken months to build the resolve to leave my safe haven for this adventure. I had not been away from home, my dogs, horse and safe routines for any significant period since my mother died. I knew it wasn't healthy, but it was what helped me stay on an even keel.

There had been more to deal with. A year after Mum passed away, my father had died of a heart attack, and I was flooded with regrets for our lost years. At his funeral I met his friends and colleagues and grasped that I barely knew him at all. Then my much-loved stepfather Lorenz had a serious stroke and cardiac arrest. Another hospital vigil had ensued. Throughout these years I had remained single. It had been tough.

I needed a break and a long one. Coming to Colorado – this was it.

I had started learning about natural horsemanship, with its emphasis on relationship, leadership and equine psychology, to help me address the remaining difficulties I was having with Winston. I had established a measure of cooperation with him but only when we did what he wanted to do.

So here I was standing in front of the log cabin that would be my home for the next six weeks. Nestled on the mountainside, amongst the trees, scrub and vegetation, it was a short walk down a track to the corralled area where the horses would be kept at night. It looked quaint, authentic and the views were the most awe-inspiring I had ever seen. I climbed the five rough wooden steps and pushed on the door to the bunkhouse. It creaked open and my bubble was burst.

Inside it was dark, the tiny window laced with dusty cobwebs. Two pairs of bunk beds, connected with crooked ladders lashed roughly together from saplings, were the only items of furniture excepting a plastic garden chair wedged in the corner. The tired mattresses on each bed were covered in dark red vinyl fabric and were ripped here and there. A tiny electric bar heater offered a glimmer of hope for cold nights and a broom handle erected across one corner of the hut boasted a few bowed wire coat hangers for storage. That was it. No wardrobes, drawers, no nothing. Where would the four of us who would be sharing put all our belongings? A single portable lantern hung on the wall to help guide us in the dark from the cabin down to the lodge, which was 10 minutes' walk away and where the wash facilities could be found. My excitement stalled. There wasn't even a toilet close to hand. What on earth had I signed up for?

I stepped out of the cabin for air. It had been muggy and musty inside. Before me, across the dark green treetops, I could see snow-capped peaks soaring against the sapphire sky. The stillness was broken by a rustling in the bushes and a deer with extraordinarily large ears stepped out into a clearing alongside the cabin. I gasped. It was only feet away and stared at me softly with big brown eyes then vanished back into the undergrowth. I recalibrated my expectations. This was going to be amazing and worth some simple living. In fact, wasn't that the whole point?

### *I meet my teacher*

After lunch on the first day it was time to go out into the dry mountain heat to have our horses allocated. I was excited to meet the one who would be mine for the duration of the programme. We were split into three groups of four, and each chattering huddle was then sent to stand by a corral containing four horses in each. I looked in at the horses next to me and wondered how they would select the right one for me: height, weight, experience perhaps?

The instructor interrupted my thoughts. 'OK, now it's time for the horses to choose you. Move into the corral and hang out with them until you've been picked.'

The horses would choose us? Not the other way around! I couldn't believe it. What if I was chosen by one of the really big ones? Worse – what if I was not chosen at all?

The first student in my group to 'click' with one of the horses put her arm over his neck proprietarily. I was relieved – his height worried me. Now there were three left. I had my eye on a small dark-brown one. I liked his size. But then another student stepped in to stroke him. I turned round.

I looked at the tall grey horse opposite me – did it look as if it liked me? I stepped hesitantly forwards but it shunned me as did the fourth horse. I knew it. None of them wanted me. Panic, shame and humiliation raced wildly around my body and to my horror, I felt a tremble in my lip. I hoped no one would notice and clenched my fists.

'Pam this is stupid. Pull yourself together!' And although it felt ridiculous to be so upset I knew it as a familiar sensation. The netball court. That was it! This is how it felt in games lessons when I was chosen last. As this memory crystallised it brought with it a moment of pure insight – how badly I wanted approval and how hard I had always worked to win it.

As I braced myself for rejection, I felt a little nudge in my back. I turned round. The shorter brown horse, who I thought had engaged with the other student, was standing right by me. I didn't know how he had got there, but there he was. I invited him to sniff my hand and when he brushed it with the soft down on his nose my skin danced. I stroked his shining, muscled neck, and at that moment we connected. To my embarrassment, I started crying. Was it with relief or gratitude?

I was handed a halter and rope by the instructor, a tall handsome Texan in crisp denim, cowboy boots, white shirt and cream Stetson. 'Looks like you've been picked, Ma'am,' he grinned. 'This horse's name is Coop. You'll find out why in due course ... Enjoy him.'

Later I would wonder why Coop came to me when he did. Was it that he was drawn to me in that moment of real authenticity when I accepted a truth about myself? Was it the intensity of my emotion? My vulnerability? Or did he sense that we would understand each other? Soon it was as if this horse had always been mine and always would be. The passing of time took on an unreal dimension and it felt as if these weeks would never end. This was now my life. For a while at least.

## 14

## *With Coop: Healed by Peacefulness*

Handsome, with a soft eye and wispy mane and tail, I found in Coop a calm steadfastness. His playfulness was only outshone by his infinite and gentle patience with me.

Named because he liked to 'fly the coop' – it was almost impossible to restrain him in the individual corrals where the horses were kept overnight. He would jump over or even crawl under the fence like a cat, grazing the skin off his knees in the process. But the rewards for him were worth it. Most mornings, as the liquid silver light of dawn broke around the pine tops and gave way to the building power of the mountain sun, I could be seen walking to the high pastures to retrieve him from his midnight feasting.

In an effort to tempt him to stay for me, I developed a routine, rising early each day and leading him to the deep meadow at the edge of the ranch, taking a coffee and a bun with me so we could breakfast together. Cushioned by the tough alpine grasses I'd sit and take in the early morning panorama of snow-capped mountains around me, with the pink, blue, white and grey hues of the huge sky reflecting across their jutting peaks. Soothed by the sound of Coop's rhythmic grazing and his grounding presence, I came to know a new kind of peacefulness. The kind that soaked into my bones. Here, with him, my anxieties were subsiding; the layers of which had built up over the years without me even noticing.

### *When calm was lost*

I was 15 years old on the day when I had stopped being calm and started getting very good at pretending to be.

After school I ambled home from the bus stop, trailing my bag heavy with homework and with strap fraying under the weight. I lifted the latch on the side gate, and walked down the side of the house to enter, as I always did, by the kitchen.

But the glass panes in the back door were smashed. Shining shards covered the tiled floor inside.

'Mum!' I pushed the door open and stepped carefully around the broken glass and crockery which had also fallen victim. I didn't know whether to shout again or not; maybe intruders were still at large. I stood still, my heart pounding in my chest, straining to hear something. Then, through the silence, I made out the low murmur of female voices coming from the sitting room. I tiptoed quickly through the hall where the trail of devastation continued, being careful not to crunch the broken china underfoot.

Then I found her, sitting head bowed. A neighbour was comforting her with both arms around her shoulders. My mother locked her sight onto mine and smiled weakly; her ashen face was swollen and her eyes were red.

There had been an anonymous phone call. My father was having an affair. He had been for years. With a friend of the family. We all used to spend time together – holidays, Christmas, birthdays. She was the wife of my dad's best friend. That's how my parents' marriage ended, and my teenage world was changed forever. Where there had been innocence, now there was loss, shame and fear.

In the days that followed, my mother became ill. She lay in bed and cried all day. I had never heard anything like it: a low moaning like an animal suffering in some dark place, rising to a wail then falling into deep rhythmic sobs. There weren't even many tears; this was a dry kind of torment. She was frail and withdrawn, even within her sturdy frame. Vitality thrived only in her bitterness that she spewed upon me as I sat in vigil loyally and gravely at her bedside. She shared the details of the affair, of how my father had been treating her those past 10 years. Sorrows a teenager should not have heard, and which broke the love I had for my father. She was taken to hospital; I can't remember for how long. My grandmother came to help us out; my dad had left. I was told that she had an infection. But later, much, much, later, I realised that she had suffered a breakdown.

### *The façade was born*

That was when I learned to cope, and when I wasn't coping, I learned to look as if I was. Terrified of upsetting my mother, or adding to her woes, I kept my grief to myself, but in reality, my world was shattered. Nothing seemed safe anymore.

I had always been conscientious and studious, a teacher's pet, as my brothers called me sometimes. I liked school, and I was also thirsty for the approval that came with good marks. So I worked hard. But now burying myself in my books, striving to do well at whatever I touched, became a way of channelling and concealing my anxiety as well as a way of being liked. Focussing on my work also helped me to forget the troubles in the family.

Thus, a pattern was set, and the façade that I continued to nurture through university was perfected by the time I entered professional life as a young woman. My bosses and peers described me as calm, competent, able to handle pressure, whilst being ambitious, hard-working and determined. That was how the world saw me and how I liked to see myself. That was what I was acclaimed and rewarded for and what I was also proud of. It did not stop me lying awake at night, worrying about whether what I had done would be good enough, or whether at some point I would be found out for the fake that I felt I was.

In my thirties, one of my professional mentors, a coach and psychotherapist, had even suggested in one of our development reviews, that I might benefit from undertaking some long-term psychotherapy. I brushed the comment off politely, yet was both scornful and unsettled by the suggestion. Me? Psychotherapy? There was nothing wrong with me! Perhaps she had seen what lay beneath my carefully constructed yet unconscious veneer. If I had taken her advice, I might have avoided the disastrous decisions that later led to so much unhappiness.

### *This moment is what counts*

One morning as Coop and I breakfasted in the grass rich with late spring flowers, I became aware that I was breathing in a new way. My lungs seemed bigger and were filling and emptying with a depth and rhythm I didn't ever remember having before. Soft, deep and long. An intense sense of well-being coursed throughout my whole body and mind. I felt entirely calm and became aware that I was no longer worried. No longer coping or pretending to cope. I was me, in a meadow, on a mountain, with this horse. I didn't particularly care about what happened the next hour, day, week or year. What I was, and felt, at that moment, was what counted.

We walked back to the ranch together, ready for our day's work, shoulder to shoulder, step matching step, my arm resting across Coop's smooth, flat, shining back. Something in me had changed. With the calmness had come acceptance of myself as I was, which brought a lightness to my soul. I also understood how healing it was to simply be peaceful.

## 15

## *The Burnout Trap*

Bridget was someone who would find, as I had with Coop, that seeking inner stillness would be the key to redefining the quality of her life and health. A glittering career had led to a position on the board of a large manufacturing company at the age of 38 where she had operated successfully for 10 years. This strident businesswoman travelled extensively with her husband looking after the home and their two children, who were now entering their teens. But in recent times, she told me, her career seemed to have ground to a halt, having been passed over twice for the role of Chief Executive. She was despondent and losing confidence and was offered coaching with the purpose of improving her chances the next time round.

We sat in the classroom, becoming acquainted shortly after her arrival.

'I feel I am on this knife-edge all the time …' Bridget's voice trembled. Her complexion was grey and pale, and her skin stretched taught across her cheek bones. 'So I work harder. But the more I do, the longer hours I work, the worse the feeling gets. And I seem less likely to get promoted now than I did two years ago. And if I don't make CEO, then I'm finished. And then what? Then what will I do? That is where my whole career has been leading. It's all I have ever wanted. But it all feels like it has been a complete waste of time.'

'And how do you hope the coaching process will help,

Bridget?' I asked.

'Well, I think what I need to focus on is better influencing skills. I feel like I'm always fighting to get myself noticed. So exploring how I can build better relationships with the chairman and non-execs, how to influence them better. That would be good.'

### *The burnout trap*

Bridget continued to talk about her life, sharing that she worked between 60 and 70 hours a week including time at the weekend, and even dialled into daily conference calls on holiday. She found it hard to switch off. The worst thing, she felt, was how grumpy she was with her husband, children, and her team at the office. The more tired she had become, the less effective she seemed to be, and the harder she felt she needed to work to stay ahead of the game. Perhaps influencing wasn't really the problem, I wondered. Bridget was describing classic symptoms of burnout.

'The pressure is massive,' she explained. 'I feel it's all going to go badly wrong at any moment. That we'll miss our targets, which will look even worse for me. I know I get stressed and can't help taking it out on other people – I get so tired of having to push the team the whole time.'

It sounded as if she demanded the same kind of commitment from her team as she gave herself. They, too, were exhausted.

As we put further definition around her desire to be more influential, the coaching process faltered.

'So, Bridget, what strategies have you tried so far with respect to influencing?'

'Er, I don't know really.'

'OK, can you describe how you have influenced people in a situation where things have gone well for you?'

'Hmmm, no not really. I can't think of one.'

'And when things have gone badly?'

'I don't know; I guess I haven't thought about it much.'

'And what would success look like for you at the end of today?'

'Er. I don't know. I haven't prepared very well, have I?'

### *An absence of clarity*

As a coach I was stumped – every exploratory question, every reflection elicited the same, flat response. She was well and truly stuck. The only thing that was clear was that for Bridget there was not much clarity. This could easily have been a result of the fatigue which weighed her down.

'OK then Bridget. Let's work with 'I don't know'. Let's explore how it is not to know, not to have clarity, and see what happens.'

In the paddock the horses didn't want Bridget anywhere near her and kept moving away. Horses need to feel safe around people, and what helps them to do so is calm, clear leadership from someone who is present – in their body as well as their mind. She was none of those things.

As their illusive manoeuvres continued, Bridget became frustrated with the horses and increasingly deflated. She kept saying, 'I don't know what to do.'

We were getting nowhere quickly, so I suggested that we do something to help her clear her mind. She readily agreed and we undertook a short meditation, standing out in the field, working on releasing the physical tension caused by her indecision. An almost imperceptible rise and fall of her shoulders suggested that perhaps the serenity of the Wiltshire hills and the steady presence of the grazing horses was sinking in. I checked in with her:

'What's happening for you right now, Bridget?'

'Do you know, I feel so much more peaceful. I'm beginning to notice how lovely it is here; how nice it is to watch the horses. I don't really feel like I need to do anything in particular with them. Think I'll stop worrying about what to do and soak in the sunshine. Is it OK if I sit down in the field and watch them?'

I nodded, and she ambled over to a sunny spot in the centre of the field, and sat legs crossed, picking daisies out from the green blanket beneath.

### Embracing stillness

Five or ten silent minutes passed until one of the ponies, Jack, took interest and ambled towards her stopping some six feet away. Remarkably he then softly touched her shoulder and lay down in the grass next to Bridget and went to sleep. The pony snored through twitching whiskers as his round fat belly heaved up and down. It was a touching and peaceful scene. Only broken when Jack's stomach rumbled and he passed wind rather dramatically. Bridget couldn't contain her hilarity.

'Well, that is what he thinks of my problems!'

She then rested back on her elbows, with the sun on her face, taking delight in the companionship of the slumbering mound beside her.

After some time, Jack raised his head and prepared to stand, gathering his legs under him and rocking gently to find his balance. I guided Bridget too to get to her feet in case he rolled too close to her as he stood up. The pony, now upright, put his head down and shook the sleep off his body from nose to tail. Bridget laughed again.

As we were summing up I noticed that she looked different and noticeably younger. 'I haven't felt like this for years,' she said. 'I'm remembering what it feels like to be me.'

We continued talking. Her limiting song, 'I don't know what to do,' had, in fact, been ringing in her ears for a long time. And it didn't only relate to how she should work with the horses or achieve promotion. Deep down, she didn't know what to do about her life, which was draining her so badly.

The relaxation techniques Bridget learned that day became a regular routine during the coming six months during which we worked together every four weeks. By making sure that she had more time off with her family and pursued leisure activities for herself, soon her relationships at home and work improved. As Bridget became calmer and less fatigued, she was better able to think through her options, and in time we progressed to work on her leadership vision, energy and purpose.

### *Calmness brings clarity*

What transpired was that deep down Bridget didn't really want to be CEO. It was her ego which coveted the top job. She had bought into the belief years earlier that making Chief Executive would represent success and to not make the grade would be failure. She was driven by the desire *not to fail*, rather than because she genuinely wished for the job. Once she had tasted what it was like to feel like herself while living in the present moment, that became her aspiration. She adjusted her priorities and applied to transfer to a role which took her closer to home so she could be actively involved in the life of her children.

A few months after her coaching process ended, Bridget chose to take on a substantial role in a smaller subsidiary of the business. It came with some challenges but was less stressful. She enjoyed more autonomy and, importantly, she was able to get home most nights at a reasonable hour.

Bridget had pursued her ambition to the point of exhaustion. She was risking everything: her health, family and credibility for something she didn't really want. While all her resources were invested in chasing her goal, she avoided confronting a truth which was uncomfortable. Choosing positively to step out of the habit of stress allowed her to do so and embrace the change which unfolded.

### *Calmness creates choice*

A relatively short time spent peacefully was enough to remind Bridget that it felt good to live in the moment instead of in her ambition. She joined a meditation group and embraced a discipline of mindfulness even if it was just for a few minutes a day. She found that the more regularly she relaxed, the more able she was to bring clarity to the dilemma she was facing, and the more choices she created for herself. She was no longer slave to her outdated aspiration.

Bridget discovered that while she was immersed in physical, emotional and mental burnout, intellectual analysis was ineffective in solving the problem of her discontent. In the grip of chronic stress her 'fight or flight' response kicked in – the more she fretted about her situation, the more stressed she got, so the less able she was to see a way out. As she became skilled at calming herself, she reached the truth about her career quickly. The 'noise' which had echoed in her mind and drove her to achieve her false goal had been preventing her from hearing the inner message which was there all along. She had to find stillness to hear that wisdom.

## *Seek rightness not right*

The need for certainty about outcomes was also preventing
Bridget from seeing the different options which could suit
her better. She was searching for the 'right' answer, thus
narrowing her field of choice. Looking for 'rightness' helped
her to adopt a more creative stance to her problem solving.
Rightness is something which is *felt* rather than *known,* so it
was only once she had tuned into her real emotional
responses that she was able to do this. Then she had been
able to ask herself questions like: 'What does this career
option bring me?' 'How will this choice serve me, my loved
ones and my purpose?' and 'Does it enable me to follow
joy?'

These kinds of questions enabled her to activate her
emotional decision-making apparatus, her intuition, by
relating her dilemma to her heart and spirit. She could then
explore the different dimensions of each choice in relation to
what would be good for her soul and her family.

## *16*

## *Coop's Lesson in Honesty*

### *Colorado, 2008*

In spite of the strong connection that we had made in the beginning, Coop began to challenge me in our second week together. A few days earlier, we had been playing in one of the round pens, a large circular enclosure with a low fence in which we could improve our communication without the need for halter and rope. I was standing in the middle of the pen asking him to trot around me in a circle. He had turned from the perimeter track where he was jogging unenthusiastically, looked me in the eye, then, spinning on his heels, had jumped right out of the pen and galloped away across the surrounding meadow. I had to giggle and accept his feedback although I wasn't quite sure what it meant.

### *Ready to learn from my guide*

I knew I had a lot to figure out. So at the first opportunity I led Coop to my favourite spot in one of the meadows at the edge of the ranch where we could linger unseen and uninterrupted. The sun was warm on the pages of my journal as I wrote and I could hear the distant buzzing of a chainsaw, bass to a melody of crickets and birdsong. Coop was 10 feet away, grazing efficiently amongst the daisies, and I could smell the sweet grass as he crushed it with his jaws.

I was realising that there was a lot more to this course

than horsemanship. My experience with Coop was leading me on the next stage of the journey that I had started with Carabella in deepest rural Spain and continued with Delilah, Gemma then Winston. The difference was that now I knew I was on a journey, and that Coop was my guide. Finally, I was ready to take all the feedback that he gave me. I was ready to learn.

### *Everything means something*

My reflections flowed from my pen and took a shape I could not deny. My ability to connect with this smart little horse was not about technique or skill; it was about how honest I was with myself. I remembered the first day in the corral when Coop picked me. He acknowledged me in the very moment that I had owned not only how I was feeling, but also the power that this emotional pattern had exerted all my life. As the self-doubt of anticipated rejection flushed through me he had nudged me gently in the small of my back. This was no coincidence. One of the instructors at the ranch had a saying he used whenever a student asked a question about their horse's behaviour: 'Everything means something, nothing means nothing.' I knew exactly now what he meant.

There was the day, too, that Coop jumped out of the corral. At the time, I wondered if he was bored with me. But when I thought about it, I had been trying to be something that I wasn't. I felt out of my depth amongst some of the other students as they rode around the ranch bareback with a mere piece of string to guide and control their horses. I needed more help with my horsemanship, but I was afraid to ask and risk looking stupid alongside these more experienced people. So I pretended instead to be confident. Coop, of course, saw through it.

### *Horses reveal our emotions*

Could it be that this horse was showing me my own emotions by revealing when I feigned to feel something different? Was he thus helping me to acknowledge how I really felt and build a clearer, deeper understanding of myself by doing so? As I explored these questions, scribbling in my notebook, the realisation grew that instead of being something shameful to hide away, my emotions could actually be useful. That if I owned them they would then run through me like ripples on the water, bringing new information, new life and energy. If I denied them, they would whisper in the shadows, controlling me, eroding my confidence and making me uncertain.

I did not realise it, that day on the mountainside, but these insights would later crystallise into a new purpose, which would take further shape over the following weeks. But perhaps it wasn't new, perhaps it had been there all the time and only now was I becoming ready to glimpse it.

## 17

## *Emotions – Friend not Foe*

Horses stay alive in the wild by sensing when they are safe and when they are not. They are highly adapted to detect anything in their environment that might jeopardise their likelihood of survival. The information they perceive includes the emotions and intentions of predators around them. They are so finely tuned that they notice and respond to human feelings before we are even aware of them ourselves. This is how they can help us to understand our inner world if we are prepared to listen. And by honing our own emotional radar we not only improve our chances of having productive relationships and increased well-being we will also be much better equipped to make good choices. Because our emotions are a source of great information and advice.

James came to work with me because he was feeling depressed, with low energy and motivation. He felt that he needed a different job, maybe a complete change of career direction, but was struggling to know for sure and it was dragging him down. During his first encounter, in spite of his prevailing humour, James built a strong and playful connection with my horse, Winston.

'That has cheered me up no end; I haven't had so much fun in ages.'

As he said goodbye his expression told me he felt uplifted. However four weeks later, when he next came to work with us, his outlook had slipped further into a world-weary lethargy.

'I'm feeling worse to be honest than I was the first time I came. I can't get a full night's sleep, don't know why, and haven't found any energy to make progress with my career decisions. It all seems too hard, too complicated. I'd like to forget my problems for a while and play with Winston again. I hate being like this – if I could enjoy myself, like last time, distract myself, then perhaps I could change my tune.'

## *Horses reveal our inner world*

But when James approached Winston, who had previously been so playful, it wasn't long before he crooked one leg and went to sleep, on all fours, as horses do. So James approached Ruby. She soon dozed off too as did Dawn and Ellie the miniature Shetland ponies. After only 15 minutes, all four of the herd were snoozing around him. James turned to me, shoulders raised and open palms outstretched quizzically. I, too, was perplexed. Trusting that the horses knew what was needed, I was guided by their response.

'Perhaps the horses are trying to tell you something, James. Maybe you could try doing what they are doing?'

So James stood next to Ruby, a flat hand supported by her back, where he rested for around 15 minutes. The herd were motionless bar the occasional nodding of their drowsy heads and flick of a tail to keep the flies off. Then one by one each of them shook off their stupor, stretched, yawned and ambled off. I eased my way over to James as the horses withdrew and we sat down in the grass to debrief:

'What emotion were you aware of as you approached the first horse to play?' I asked.

'I was excited, looking forward to playing again.'

'And how did you notice that in your body? What were

the physical sensations that went with it?'

James paused, for quite a while, searching for his answer. 'Hmmm. When I think about it, I thought I was excited, but what I was physically feeling was numbness. And I had heavy legs; that was mostly what I was aware of.'

'And what about the signs you might associate with excitement? Did you have those?'

'No, I didn't have that tingling in my stomach or liveliness that usually goes with being excited. Perhaps I felt like I *ought* to be excited because last time it was such a laugh and I did so well.'

'Think again, what was the emotion you were feeling as you approached the horses?'

'I guess a bit sad, depressed. I have been feeling quite desperate lately, not knowing what to do to make my work life happier. But now I am too tired for that even.'

'That sounds quite different to being excited ...'

'Well, no one likes to say they are depressed do they? Or down or worried. Not at work, especially. People think you're weak.'

'And if it could be OK to say that is how you really feel, could you draw a lesson from the emotions you were feeling?'

'Perhaps I need to look after myself. First and foremost. Take a break. Stop worrying for a while.'

### *Emotions help us to be who we are*

James's conclusion that day helped him to take some time out from work. His company granted him a month off during which time he focussed on spending time with his growing family. He eventually decided to reconnect with a passion of his, which was fine art, and signed up for an Open University course. His employers offered study leave although James had to fund the project himself. He did not have to leave his job or the organisation he liked. The stimulus of doing something that fed his soul was enough to reignite his enthusiasm for life and work.

James had found it difficult to own his low mood, perhaps due to the real or imagined taboo surrounding depression in his workplace, or the significant investment he had made in an alternative persona. The horses' authentic response to his frame of mind helped him to tune into the simple yet powerful message therein. By tuning into his emotions James was able to not only make a good choice to address his lifestyle – but one which helped him get closer to who he really was.

## *18*

## *Emotions at Work*

When a slim, pale and anxious man stepped into the room I could not have been more surprised. The Human Resources Director of the large organisation where John was working at a senior level had spoken to me at length about this referral. He had been accused of bullying by someone in his team. Careful mediation had avoided a formal complaint and John had agreed to have some coaching to help him change his leadership style and build more effective and respectful relationships. He spoke softly and struggled to contain his emotion as he shared the sequence of events that had led up to the accusation. He had never had any problems with any of his teams in the past, on the contrary, he prided himself on how much he valued people and the importance of winning their commitment. He was adamant that he detested the kind of intimidating behaviour he found himself being blamed for, having had a rough time at school from some of the older boys.

'I have always seen myself as a people person,' he said, 'that is why this has knocked me for six so badly. Can I have been so wrong in my assessment of my own qualities? Can I really be so bad at my job? I don't have any confidence in myself anymore.'

### *Bullying? Really?*

As we explored his values and a full picture of his working life, I became increasingly unsure about what had caused John's relationship with his colleague to unravel so badly. He presented as a kind and thoughtful person. He articulated clearly what it took to be an effective, emotionally intelligent leader, and he had good role models. He described a supportive, stable family at home. Bullying? Really?

Suspending my judgement one way or another, I suggested that we might meet the horses, to get a break from talking. I noticed that my own energy had dipped, and I was feeling on edge. Quite possibly I was resonating with John's own state.

'How are you right now, John?' I asked, as we stopped at the gate to the paddock where Winston and Ruby were grazing.

'I'm fine,' he said.

'What kind of fine? Can you describe it for me?' I asked.

'Fine. I feel OK.'

'OK,' I said, 'and how do you feel about working with the horses? You said that you hadn't been around any before ...?' I left the phrase hanging, and it stretched slowly into an uncomfortable silence. John shifted his weight from one foot to the other.

'I suppose I am a bit nervous, they look quite big.'

'And how are you noticing that nervousness in your body? What does it feel like?'

'You know, sweaty palms, butterflies, that kind of thing.'

'OK, I'm going to share a relaxation exercise which might help.'

I invited him to close his eyes and feel the weight of his body drop down through his hips and knees into his feet, making sure they were firmly on the ground. Guiding him then to release tension from his muscles each time he breathed out I brought his awareness to the beauty of nature around us, the birdsong, the rustle of the breeze in the trees and the lilting sound of the horses munching the grass.

Gently, and trying not to interrupt the serenity of the moment, I continued:

'John, shall we go into the paddock now?'

'Yes, ok ... I do hope they like me.'

### The silent story

Stepping through the gate I noticed John's breath had become shallow again, and his knuckles were white around tight fists. Both Ruby and Winston ignored him as he approached, then when he was about six feet away gradually distanced themselves from him. His frame visibly crumpled in front of me.

'What is happening for you, John?'

'I knew they wouldn't like me. I feel stupid now. I should be able to do this; it can't be that hard.'

I encouraged him to keep breathing and noticing what he felt the sense of his emotions was, as he reapproached the horses. They carried on moving away. I wondered whether he would turn to me for help. He didn't and unexpressed frustration mounted. I checked in with him again, with the same question.

'What's happening, now, John?'

'Well, they obviously don't like me.'

'And what else?'

'I knew this would happen. They are too busy eating.'

I had hoped to hear something different from John, but he was not yet connecting with the anger and frustration which was taking the place of his initial concerns. I could sense it; the horses could. But John could not. And the more frustrated he became, the more they evaded him.

## *Emotional blindness*

Eventually, he stormed up to me. 'This is pointless!'

His tone was reproachful. I paused to let the sting of his exclamation wash over me then encouraged, 'Say some more about that John?'

'I am so frustrated! What's the point of this? I could scream and shout at those stupid horses!'

Finally, we had got there. I asked John if he would like to let off some steam.

'How will that help?' he snapped.

'You might feel better. Go on, have a rant, try it. Rant as if no one is watching.'

Like a truculent schoolboy, he marched about the field, muttering ferociously under his breath. When he got back to me his face had come alive with expression and he was standing taller. He seemed more calm. Ruby and Winston were looking at him intently, with their ears pricked forwards.

'Have you seen that?' I asked, pointing towards them.

He turned, and seeing their eager faces, 'Well I never!'

'They might like to meet you now,' I suggested.

He ambled over and both horses stood while he offered a hand in humble greeting. His touch accepted, he smoothed their powerful necks one at a time.

A short time later we sat with a mug of tea each on the grassy bank adjacent to the paddock and explored what had unfolded. I helped John to track his experience at an emotional, mental and physical level. He realised that when he entered the field he was fearful, not of the horses hurting him, but of rejecting him. As his sureness disintegrated he didn't ask for help, or look for other options, he kept trying the same thing even though it hadn't worked. Each time the horses walked away, his frustration escalated until in the end he exploded and burst out full of scorn for them. It was all *their* fault.

'And does this situation feel familiar at all, John?' I asked gently.

He went quiet. 'Oh, gosh. Yes, it does. Now I see ...' I allowed silence to enfold this precious insight. He drew a deep breath.

'I guess I do tend to keep the lid on things. Especially if I am feeling out of my depth or at odds with someone. Then it all builds up, until the pressure cooker blows.'

'And did you notice, how at the end, when you were expressing and owning your frustration, this was a lot easier for the horses? They didn't seem to mind it at all when you stomped and cursed around the field, when your behaviour matched your feelings. It was when you suppressed your emotions that they stayed away. Horses pick that up because when we bottle things up, we tighten our muscles to keep it all in check. People notice too, even at an unconscious level. We just don't give the human race credit for such sensitivity.'

John nodded gravely and dropped his head into his hands as he accepted the difficult possibility that although his intention had not been to harass his colleague, it could very well have felt like that for them.

### *Physical awareness of emotional experience*

John returned several times to continue his progress with the horses and learned to tune in much earlier to his feelings by noticing the physical sensations as they originated in his body. The enhanced personal awareness which this engendered yielded a better understanding of his responses to other people. When he yearned for approval, for example, this could indicate that he needed more support from, or to build common ground with, a colleague. Perhaps at those vulnerable times he could also be kind to himself and acknowledge that some of his insecurity belonged to another time and place, many years ago, when he was bullied at school. When he was frustrated, perhaps rather than scolding himself with 'shoulds' and 'shouldn'ts' it could indicate that he needed to look for a different solution or ask for help. Perhaps if he allowed his emotions to guide him like this, John absorbed that he could avoid the suppressed frustration which periodically made him so volatile.

The key for John in understanding the cause and effect of his erratic behaviour was tuning into his emotional experience somatically, and accepting it as his own so he could use it productively. The powerful reactions that were sparked when he felt rejected linked back to his days at school when he was bullied himself. Being unpopular had been dangerous, humiliating, even terrifying. No wonder that it was hard to acknowledge these sentiments, and that instead he pretended to be 'fine'. Although he had never intended to bully anyone – far from it – what bubbled beneath the surface distorted the non-verbal impact he had on others.

In the same way that Coop enabled me to take responsibility for the parts of my inner story of which I was least proud, Winston and Ruby helped John to understand the enduring impact of his early life experiences. He was then able to find compassion both for himself and for the colleague he had wounded and rebuild their relationship, alongside his own confidence and self-esteem.

## 19

### *Coop: The Challenge of Trusting*

**Colorado, 2008**

In my third week with Coop, the progress I had been making following the insights achieved in the meadow dissolved – my riding was a disaster. I yearned to find harmony in the saddle but I felt more like a sack of potatoes bouncing around on Coop's back. Patiently he would stop, wait while I regained my balance, and then off we'd go again. Bounce, stop, wait, start, bounce, stop, wait. I knew the problem was muscle tension in my body, creating a physical and emotional brace in my horse. But try as I might to relax I still couldn't.

One evening, I was sitting out on the terrace of the lodge, a large wooden building that served as classroom, canteen and social space for the students at the ranch. I was watching the sun set behind the peaks on the far horizon, the sky ablaze with shades of peach, orange, muted blue, grey and the occasional dark cloud that might later shed large luscious raindrops on the higher slopes. Hummingbirds whose bright colours bewitched me were drinking their final draught of the day from the nectar feeders swinging in the breeze, their wings beating so fast they were a blur around their tiny bodies. As night fell and the full moon cast its silver sheen across the treetops, it came to me.

## *Accepting a difficult truth*

How could I possibly relax the physical brace in my body when emotionally I was as rigid as a plank? To relax, I had to feel safe, and I didn't. But I knew that Coop was kind and reliable. So why didn't I? I pondered. I had to admit that this was not about my horse. It was myself I doubted. But was that all?

I searched my conscience and uncovered that I had other unpleasant emotions at play too. Envy was way up there, of some of the other students who were so much better than me, who had grown up riding horses and made it all look so easy. Why couldn't I be like them? I shuddered also to acknowledge that I couldn't help feeling resentment at Coop – a lesser part of me blamed him for my lack of success. Yet the loudest echo of all in my mind was a voice saying, 'What's the point of all this anyway? Because soon you'll have to go home and get back to work. Instead of playing around pretending to be a cowgirl.' My self-critic was having a ball.

I had always seen myself as a positive person. Without an optimistic spirit I might not have survived what I had. But now I had to challenge my self-perception. I was caught up in some debilitating negativity. It was hard to accept this part of me which felt so ugly as well as the other aspects that I liked: the optimist, the caring daughter, respected boss, the listener, the woman who was always ready with a smile for others. But I realised that unless I did, I was surely not going to do justice to this amazing horse or get the most out of this once-in-a-lifetime experience. It was time to step up and face the truth about myself that Coop was revealing.

### *Trusting means being vulnerable*

To change how I was relating with my situation, first I knew I simply had to be aware of what was going on for me. Then I had to accept how I was and cease judging myself so harshly. I had to stop comparing myself to others – they had their journey and I had mine. And when it came to riding, above all, I would have to trust the two of us: me *and* Coop. And not only with my mind, I would have to surrender my whole self to the experience we were going to have together. Until I did I'd be that sack of potatoes. I had to allow myself to become vulnerable with him, and rest in the conviction that our relationship was strong. Most of all though I had to be the positive person, at my core, that I liked to project to the world, but which, at times, was only skin deep.

The next day, I saddled up as usual and rode to a corner of the ranch. I asked Coop to trot, consciously placing my faith in him by leaving the reins loose on his neck. I put to one side thoughts of equestrian technique and simply focussed on allowing myself to be carried by the horse beneath me, while ensuring that I kept breathing deeply. I imagined connecting softly with him through my seat bones and my hands which rested on the fine silk of his mane. Soon we established a steady, regular rhythm making great circles in the expansive meadow; I moved in harmony with Coop and he maintained his pace. It felt good, and I knew this was the moment when there could be no holding back.

I tied the reins to the high pommel on the front of the intricately carved Western saddle and after stroking Coop's shoulder and murmuring reassurance let my hands and arms hang softly at my side. I dared not consider that not only was I riding without reins, but I was in a vast open space a long way from the nearest fence. Coop lowered his head and I heard him blow out, enthusiastically clearing his air ways. A sign of relaxation. I felt that we were truly connected and I could rely on him absolutely. I would let him decide how and where we went. As we reached an upward slope, he broke into a canter, pounding the pasture beneath. Then, as the gradient smoothed his supple body flattened and stretched beneath me into the exhilarating four beats of a gallop. I resisted the temptation to grab the reins and stop him and instead let out a loud, 'Whoop, whoop!' It felt like my spirit had been set free to run with his. At the brow of the hill, he came to a gentle stop. We were heaving for breath. I leaned forward, stroking his solid neck, and raised my victorious fists to the sky 'We did it! We bloody well did it!'

I had caught a glimpse of what it felt like to truly believe in myself. Now, anything at all was possible.

## 20

## *Vulnerability and Change*

It was easy to see that Trevor was popular; he made people laugh and engaged readily with those he had not met before. He presented as a successful, powerful individual with a booming voice and easy humour. With a dozen of his colleagues he had come to work with me as part of a company-wide leadership development programme that his employers were sponsoring.

In spite of his amiable rapport with his colleagues, the different horses he worked with on the first morning all gave him a wide berth. Something about him made them uncomfortable. I noted that he had deflected feedback from both the horses and his colleagues albeit with humour.

### *Ego resisted*

After lunch, the small group he was working with were tasked with moving two horses from one paddock to the next via a twisting and turning course. When it was Trevor's turn to lead one of the ponies, Star, he took the rope and held it short and tight in spite of the guidance he had been given to the contrary. The pony looked warily out of the side of his eye and took a few steps before squarely planting his feet. He was not going to give an inch.

I tactfully reminded Trevor not to drag on the rope yet still he clung onto it. Unsurprisingly the pony continued to resist movement, chin defiantly pushed forwards.

Eventually, Trevor launched the rope at Beth one of his colleagues.

'You try! I give up!'

Beth responded gracefully and spent some time stroking and talking with Star. When she moved off to walk around the course he followed her willingly.

Trevor fell silent and when Beth rejoined the group he found it hard to congratulate her. Easier was to hypothesise as to why the pony would not follow him but did her. I said nothing and let him finish.

'So would you like to try again, Trevor, and if so what will you do differently, having observed Beth?' I was surprised when he said:

'Yes, that'd be great to have another go and prove I can do it. This time I will be more firm, I'll put my foot down.' No one in the group spoke, nor I. After a short silence, I then asked if the situation felt familiar at all.

'Yes, it does, funny you should say that! At work, though, I wouldn't wait so long to be more demanding with people!'

'I was also curious, how it was for you that your colleague succeeded where you had not, in that last activity? I noticed that you did not congratulate her or offer her feedback.'

Trevor paused and eyed me up. He twigged – I was trying to lead him somewhere with my questions. He was quiet for a moment, weighing up how to respond. The way he swallowed visibly before speaking suggested he had chosen honesty.

'Actually, it didn't feel great, I've got to admit. I felt like I must have looked stupid. Couldn't even get a tiny pony to move. Then I suppose I was a bit annoyed that Beth managed to do it almost straight away. My ego felt wounded … I'm sorry, Beth, it wasn't fair of me to withhold on you like that. You did really well … I guess I'm not comfortable in this situation where I don't really know what I'm doing. I feel out of my depth.'

'What do you do at work in similar situations?'

'Well, it doesn't happen that often, but ... hmmm ... I suppose I tend to do the same as I did with the pony. I take over, try to push people around, in a good natured jolly sort of way. Try to solve problems on my own.'

'So what other options might you have? Maybe you could use this opportunity with Star to be a little experimental?'

### *Learning to ask for help*

Trevor became thoughtful. 'I could ask for help, I suppose. That would be a first!'

'How would it be, then, to try again but to ask for help earlier, instead of putting your foot down later?'

Trevor went back into the paddock, inviting Beth to accompany him. They whispered together for a while before she stepped back, leaving him alone with the pony. He began rubbing the crest of Star's neck. But instead of attaching the rope to the pony's halter to try leading him again, Trevor walked away and sat on a log at the other side of the field, his back towards the group.

The pony followed the man with his eyes and stared fixedly at him as his face fell into his cupped hands. It was as if everyone held their breath wondering what would happen. Star dropped his head slightly, stepped forwards and ambled to within a few feet of Trevor. Then, in an extraordinarily direct gesture, bent to ruffle the man's hair with his curious lips. They stayed there motionless, apart from the swish of the pony's tail, for five or ten minutes. I saw both man and pony sigh deeply, then Star gradually departed and went back to grazing. The work was done.

Trevor had discarded his mantle of invincibility in order to ask for and accept help in front of his colleagues. By sitting down so close to the pony, he also made himself vulnerable. He trusted the pony and me to keep him safe. I felt it was no coincidence that the connection was possible with Star in that moment. Nor that during the rest of the programme, and I hope afterwards, his boldness dispersed, and he was able to be more authentically himself.

For Trevor, dropping his defences was the catalyst for changing the quality of his relationships that day and I imagined later on at work and home too. It didn't only enable change, it *was* the change he was looking for. Bringing transformation into our lives requires this of all of us because by embracing the new, we open ourselves up to risk whether that is of a financial, emotional, physical or spiritual nature. Without the courage to become vulnerable in this way, we deny ourselves the prize of personal growth and abundance.

## 21

*Coop's Inspiration: Daring to Dream*

### Colorado, 2008

It was our last week at the ranch. Since the day we galloped up the mountain, my relationship with Coop had blossomed and with it my confidence in myself and in him. I had even ridden him around the ranch bareback, my legs dangling softly at his side, each of us grounded in a relaxed kind of companionship. We were at one together. Each day began with our shared breakfast in the meadow and ended with me hugging him in his pen on the way from the washroom up to my cabin. He was the first thing that greeted me each morning and the last thing I saw at night before sinking into a deep and soulful sleep. I could never remember having been so happy, having felt so good in my body, my mind and my spirit. I could not remember, ever, having breathed so deeply from a relaxed and flexible diaphragm. Only now was I understanding that perhaps for most of my life, I had held my breath.

### Dream big, like a child

With only three days left together, all the students gathered in the lodge for the morning class. Our instructors asked us to buddy up with a partner and then played us a video clip from the film *The Black Stallion*. The clip shows the black stallion, the equine hero of the film, and a boy of around nine years old having a magical encounter on a white tropical sandy beach. They have been shipwrecked there together. They meet and make a connection, and eventually the stallion invites the boy to climb onto his back. The child, giggling, takes hold of a clutch of mane, and the great black horse gallops through the shallows of the clear green sea, with his small charge squealing in delight. The boy falls a couple of times into the water and the horse stops to pick him up. The stuff of childhood fantasies indeed. Moved and inspired, we were then asked to share our own dream with each other. We were invited to think big like the boy had. Don't settle for the ordinary, go for the extraordinary, they said. Be wild, be bold, be ambitious, be free.

My partner went first, painting a passionate picture of how she wanted to move west, find a place for her, her kids, her mom and their horses and start a leather-crafting business. Get away from the memories of her unhappy marriage. She had been through a rough divorce, wanted a fresh start. I hugged her; I knew how she felt. Then she dried her eyes and said, 'Go on, your turn.' My vision had already been forming tentatively over the past few weeks. Now I dared to verbalise it.

'I want to help people to change their lives,' I said. 'To help them be their best self and to be happy – with the help of horses. I don't know exactly what it will look like, but horses have taught me so much I don't see why it shouldn't work for everyone else. And why should only people who own horses get to benefit from their incredible spirit and presence?'

Inviting my leadership coaching clients, who I normally met in their office, or my therapy clients who I saw in a warm and cosy consulting room, to interact in the outdoors with my horses – it sounded pretty crazy even to me. But I also knew it could work.

## *The thrill of a purpose born*

The next day, I sat at lunch with a man called Ron. Most conversation on the ranch was about horses and our learning and there was a tacit agreement that no one ever talked about work or the demands of the real life we would return to at the end of the course. So it was unusual that I asked him what he did for a living.

'I'm an equine assisted therapist,' he said briskly.

I couldn't believe what I was hearing. 'Oh right – tell me some more about that.'

'My wife and I have a ranch, and we work with young people and kids with behavioural and emotional challenges. They work with the horses for therapy.'

So I wasn't crazy. People were already doing what I had talked about! My stomach turned with excitement. This wasn't a whim: it was my purpose which was taking shape.

I finished lunch and went out to meet Coop for our afternoon of riding. I was smiling inside like you do when you know a really good secret. I had decided. When I got home, I was going to reach for my dream. Why would I not?

With the thrill of my intent moving within me, I saddled up Coop and headed off for our lesson. It was led by the handsome, gracious Texan in his impeccable cream Stetson who had overseen the pairing of the horses and students on our first day. After half an hour, he asked me how the lesson was going.

'Great,' I said. 'But it's not really what I want to be doing.'

'I see, Ma'am.' He was amused. 'So what do you want to be doing?'

'I want to ride like a cowboy, enjoy Coop – let him have some fun too. It is nearly time to go home, and I haven't roped any cows yet.'

The instructor, who was mounted on his own horse, with hands crossed over the tall pommel of his Western saddle, roared.

'Well, you're riding the right horse for that. I don't know about roping cows, but let's show you what Coop can do.'

He taught me how to turn on the spot with Coop, gallop, and slide to a stop like I had seen the cowboys do when they round up the steers. Coop leapt from left to right and right to left like an agile cat. Bred for speed and agility he knew exactly how this game was played and loved it. Soon we were both breathless and united in our entertaining antics. I understood what it was to allow a horse to express himself. I had never been able to do that before.

And to do this, I had demonstrated absolute faith in Coop. I had also said quite clearly what I wanted. And to have it I had finally shed the worrisome mantle which Winston had first revealed to me.

I hosed Coop down and we went to sit in our meadow together. Looking out across the mountains, taking in the magnificence of this country and the enormity of the learning I had achieved over those 6 weeks, I decided that I would not ride him again before I went home. I would savour the time I had with him, but I wanted that day to be our last experience riding, so perfect had it been. Me, the cowgirl, and Coop.

### *At peace with being me*

That evening, I looked out across the trees and watched the coral glow of the day ebb away. I did not want it to end, it had been full of such happiness. But little by little the sun disappeared behind the mountains, leaving the sky awash with a silver sheen, which slowly dissolved into shades of burning embers. Then, within a few minutes, it was as if the lights had gone out. The sky became dark black; there was no moon that night in the magnificent sky swathed with streaks of bright stars. As I reflected on the day's events with Coop, my breath was long, slow and deep. In that moment, I felt, 'Gosh, this is me. This is what it feels like to simply be me. And this is how it feels to be at peace with being me.' It was a new feeling. I have never forgotten that moment, it serves as a reminder and a beacon when I need it.

## 22

## *Coop: Saying Goodbye*

The last day of my six-week adventure came too soon. Bags were packed, contact details exchanged, gifts purchased for friends and family back home. Those of us who had leased horses from the ranch had developed strong bonds with them and were silently dreading this morning when we would have to give them back. We had lived alongside our borrowed friends and looked after them like our own day in, day out, for the duration.

We had been asked to bring the horses down to the corral area at 10am. I couldn't speak for fear of breaking down. We followed the instructor who led us on foot across the ranch and up to the twenty sloping acres of the top pasture which nestled beneath the lower treeline of the mountain. Here the ranch horses lived as a herd in their leisure time and became shiny and round on summer grass. There were a dozen or so horses still up there who had not been needed for our programme; they were grazing at the uppermost corner. We all passed through the wide gate and were asked to space ourselves in a line with our horses in front of us; their heads tilted towards us and with our backs to the fence. On command from the instructor, we were to undo the halters and slip them off in unison whilst stepping back simultaneously. He knew what would happen, and this was to keep us all safe.

The signal came and we moved away from the horses.

For a split second, they hovered. Were they free to go or not? Coop tilted his muzzle towards me momentarily and looked with his soulful brown eyes. A moment of connection. Then, dropping his weight onto his sturdy hindquarters, he sprung straight into a gallop, as did his herd-mates, and they flew up the hill to join their friends. There were bucks, flicks, leaps, spins, sprints, stops. To see them running free like that made me gasp. The horses we had released merged with the others and they galloped around the meadow in unison, setting up a huge cloud of dust. Wheeling and swerving and swooping up and around the hillside like a grounded flock of starlings, changing patterns, shape and speed. What energy, beauty, power and grace. Coop could now have his moment to be a horse again, for a while, until the next eager student turned up.

After a while, their playtime ended and the herd meandered peacefully as they ate. I saw a pale grey horse ambling down the hill towards me. At first I didn't recognise him, then became aware that actually it was Coop. He had rolled in the chalky dust and now resembled a flour-coated version of himself. Even his eyelashes were tipped with powdery blobs like a snowy mascara. I laughed, he looked so funny. He came to me at the fence and rested the moleskin softness of his chin on my outstretched hand. 'Thank you,' I whispered. He stayed a short while blowing his warm breath into my hands then stepped sideways to drink thirstily from the trough, his dusty ears moving back and forwards as he swallowed. Then he spun on his heels and trotted away to join the herd.

It was over. It was time to go home and back to reality. But it was also time to embrace the aspiration which was forming like a warm, solid presence in my gut. I would discover over the coming years that staying on course would not be easy and that I would need resilience, patience, determination, and focus. But I would also be rewarded as the true nature of the horse would continue to be revealed.

I considered how my sense of myself had unfolded here in this mountain paradise. It had sometimes been tough. Coop had shown me that horses respond to the energy that comes from your heart, your passion and your purpose. They resonate with your spirit and how alive it is. Coop initially could not see mine at all. It had flickered and died little by little over the previous years. This had not always been the case – I started out differently – fresh and full of hope, creativity and innocence, an adventurous, spirited, joyful girl. Where had she gone?

She was emerging again with the help of Coop. I was done pretending. There was no one I had needed to please, other than my horse. And what he had wanted was simply for me to be true to myself. And the closer I got to connecting again with my essence, the more he sought me out. Instead of running away from me, he stayed and invited me to play, following my suggestions, ears pricked and eyes bright.

It seemed so clear to me then, that for all those years my main purpose had been to prove myself against someone else's standards and to win approval. If I didn't need to do that anymore could sharing the wisdom of horses with the wider world be my new raison d'etre?

As I lingered at the gate and watched the herd of horses continuing to play and graze together, I hovered at the edge of this new dawning. I didn't know what I would do when I got home. I didn't know which way my life would go. But something significant had changed for me. Being in this place of 'don't know' held excitement and promise, whereas before it had always been frightening.

## 23

## *Committing to Purpose*

When I returned from Colorado, my burgeoning mission to share the gifts of the horse was burning brightly. Decisively I set about turning it into reality. Owning one horse and with no suitable facilities to receive clients, it wasn't immediately obvious how I would establish any kind of business along the lines I was thinking of. So I set about talking and writing about what I wanted to do. When I had the opportunity to present an article for the journal of a professional association for therapists of which I was a member I jumped at the chance.

In the piece I revealed the developmental themes I encountered personally while in Colorado and drew parallels between the principles of body psychotherapy and how working with horses could help people therapeutically. I also wrote something for a leadership journal, positioning 'horse-work' as a powerful way to develop presence, impact and relational skills for leaders.

I surprised myself by being so willing to share my aspirational purpose and ideas publicly. I risked people knowing if I had failed which unnerved me. Yet at the same time, I knew that having committed ink on paper, black on white, I was giving myself no way back. Now I had to carry on.

Notwithstanding that, I was surprised when people not only read my articles but also offered encouragement and support. I half expected people to think I was a little unhinged. I certainly didn't think anyone would remember what I had written. Then a few months later at a networking lunch, I met someone who did. She introduced herself. 'I'm Lindsay, I wrote to you after I read your article, I liked it so much.'

I remembered the email, and we had an animated discussion about how horses could help young people in particular. Lindsay worked for a mental health charity supporting children and adolescents in Cambridgeshire. We stayed in touch in the weeks to come and built plans for a therapeutic project with horses for her clients. All we needed was some funding to do it.

### *The dream becomes reality*

To my delight some months later I received an email from Lindsay. She had successfully secured a budget. We would design and run a programme together with the horses. We called it Summer School.

## 24

## *Seen by a Horse*

The first thing I noticed about him were his piercings – in his nose, both ears and several in top and bottom lips. I could see tattoos peeping out from under the curling lip of his hoodie where it fell against his neck. He dragged his feet as he walked, shoulders hunched and eyes cast to the ground. His skin was grubby with pimples. Hair combed but could have done with a wash. He was rather taller than I expected too. I found him intimidating. In his early teens, he had been referred as a last attempt to get him back into a school. He had been excluded several times already for aggressive behaviour. This really was his last chance, I had been told.

'Hi Mark,' I greeted, 'I'm Pam.'

'Hi,' he replied, staring at the ground and kicking the dirt with his worn-out trainers. Was the tone sullen, or perhaps despairing? Everything about his demeanour suggested that would be the only thing he would say so I suggested that we all went to meet the horses straight away. On arriving at the paddock, I invited the young man to enter the field when he felt ready.

After five minutes, hands stuffed deep in pockets, breath high in his chest, Mark opened the gate and stepped into the paddock. The horse nearest to him, an old white gelding with a kind and curious temperament, interrupted his grazing to lift his substantial head. Mark jumped back and swore under his breath. We stood in silence and waited. I resisted the urge to offer help, sensing that it would be better if Mark asked if he wanted it. After a few minutes, he took another step forward. This time the horse took a step forwards. The tall boy turned and ran to the gate, closing it behind him, and stood for a few moments, shifting his weight awkwardly from one foot to the other. The horse nonchalantly went back to grazing. Eventually, I offered:

'Ask if you need anything from me, Mark, won't you?'

He hesitated. A few minutes elapsed.

I tried again. 'What would you like to happen right now?'

'Dunno really. Never been near a horse. Bit scared s'pose … I'd like to stroke him, though. I think. But don't think he likes me. He lunged at me before.'

'I don't believe he was intending to hurt you, that's for sure. I felt he was being friendly.'

'What if I scare him?'

'OK – if he is afraid he will look after himself. But let me share something with you which will help you reassure him. What they like is when we are relaxed; it helps if we make sure we carry on breathing. They don't like it when we hold our breath. I wonder if you might have been?'

'Dunno.'

'And is there anything else which would help you to have what you want? Anything else you would like from me?'

'Can you come in with me?' he paused. 'Please?'

'No problem, where would you like me to stand?'

'Right behind me, that'd be good … er … thanks. What's his name?'

'Oby.'

Mark re-entered the paddock with me on his heels; I reminded him to breathe as deeply as he could. He walked up slowly to the white horse calling him by name. This time, Oby stayed still and met Mark's outstretched hand with the gentlest of pressure from his nose. The corners of the young man's mouth curled.

'I think it'd be OK for you to stroke him now; now that he has said hello to you. I think he would probably like that,' I guided.

The boy stretched his tattooed hand out onto the muscled, powerful neck of the horse, and stroked him softly. I placed the grooming kit nearby, and Mark picked up a soft brush. He used it tentatively at first and then with more confidence. A new light came into his eyes as he swept the bristles across the shining coat for almost an hour in contented silence.

The next time he came Mark chose to work with Oby again, once more spending a lot of time grooming. Then he led him around the field from one delicious patch of grass to the next, asking us occasionally if what he was doing was OK. Here and there the old horse would nuzzle him affectionately, drawing a chuckle and a half-hearted reprimand:

'Oi Oby – that's my sleeve you're slobbering on!'

The third visit came, and Mark had still not said much while he was with us. I would check in with him from time to time, to ask how he was, did he need anything? He didn't; he was fine. But thank you, I appreciate that, he said at last. Words I felt he may not have uttered for quite a while. To see the way he was with the horse, so gentle and tender, it was hard to believe that the aggressive person who had been described to me even existed.

The fourth and final appointment with Mark came, and as he resumed his habitual grooming of Oby's muscled flank, a conversation grew. Although I was there alongside him, it was as if the boy was really talking to the horse. It was a monologue, an emptying, which didn't need any input from anyone else. About his brother who dealt in drugs, his mother who was an alcoholic, about his neighbourhood where street culture pervaded and he had already chosen his gang, because that was how it was done. And he also talked about

114

how he loved animals. How he longed for a dog of his own, how the best he had managed was keeping beetles in a matchbox when he was a kid. And how he adored his little sister and tried to protect her, look after her, keep her safe from bullying. He couldn't bear the idea of her growing up to be the way he was. I could imagine how tender he might be with this little girl, how much he loved her, by the way he had interacted with the horse.

But who else, anywhere, saw this boy? The real one? Or allowed, rewarded or acknowledged his kind spirit and loving nature? The version of him that the world saw, which had been created to survive in his environment; this was how he was being defined. This was all I had seen too with my human eyes when I first beheld his physical self. But not Oby, this old horse had seen the person Mark really was and reached out to befriend him.

I listened gravely to what he shared, and at the end of that last afternoon we spent together, we sat in the grass warmed from the sun. His previously pallid face had taken on a pinkish hue around his glistening eyes. I was full of sadness to see him go back to the life he had, leaving this happy moment behind him.

'Mark, thank you for showing me and Oby your kindness, gentleness, respect. He's particularly enjoyed having you here, looking after him so carefully and lovingly as you have. It's been a real privilege to witness you both together. I wish you well, and hope that the rest of the world can see very soon what we have.'

Mark said goodbye and, holding his head high, walked towards the gates of the farm. I hoped for him that he had got to know his best self well enough with Oby to be that person at his new school. Long enough for someone else to notice and help him to nurture it before it was squashed.

Mark had created a different version of himself in order

to survive his environment. For different reasons, at a different time, I knew I had done similarly in spite of my privileged middle class upbringing. I had looked in the mirror one day and simply did not recognise who I saw. Horses, though, had guided me back to myself and now they were teaching me how I could help them to do the same for others.

I watched the boy leave. He was still wearing his hoody. But the hood was down.

# 25

## *A Team Moves from Fear to Authenticity*

As well as collaborating with Lindsay on psychotherapeutic projects, I had found a business partner with whom I could work on leadership and team development programmes. I had met her at one of the conferences I attended on equine assisted learning when I returned from Colorado. We hit it off immediately and over the coming months, we planned our enterprise. It wasn't long before we were opening the doors to groups from a range of different companies. It soon became evident that the kind of insecurity which had driven Mark to construct a robust defensive persona wasn't only alive and kicking on the back streets of the inner city. It was prospering equally in the Board Room.

### *An organisation in crisis*

Stress levels were already high when the senior leadership team arrived on a balmy morning in August. In the throes of a takeover, the financial services company they were responsible for was in chaos. Sales and cost reduction targets had been increased, processes were being merged, and everyone's job was on the line. All the directors were working extensive hours, tempers were often short and emotions high. Their operational teams were all working equally hard. Employees were as afraid of potential redundancy as their leaders and morale was low. No one could afford to fail, or be seen to be dispensable. Cooperation was collapsing into competition and conflict across the business as one department blamed the next for problems occurring. As performance standards plummeted, customer complaints were on the up and profitability was on the way down. It wasn't a healthy picture for the business or anyone in it.

As the team began the day and shared what they each wanted to get out of the programme, discussion often got sucked back to work issues, focussing on everything that was going wrong. No-one listened, interruption and disagreement were common and humour, badly disguised as good-natured banter, was used to deflect feedback or undermine others. Although these men and women had come willingly, I felt that in reality they were reluctant to talk freely. I was not surprised – who knew what might happen once their Pandora's box was opened.

After the introductions it was time to meet the herd. The men and women walked out from the classroom towards the paddocks. They were chatting animatedly in pairs and seemed unaware of their environment or the horses who were now walking purposefully, one after the other, to the furthest corner of the field. From there they continued grazing with a wary eye on the group. One at a time the members of the team tried to approach the herd all of whom remained elusive. After some discussion a decision was made to reorganise and see if going in pairs would help. But to no avail, all they saw of the equines were their swinging tails as they left.

When eventually the team decided that they needed to sit down, away from the horses, to discuss how they were going to win their confidence, the unhelpful ways in which they behaved towards each other became steadily more clear. Criticism and blame were dished out with no one willing to accept responsibility for what was a collective lack of success and the good suggestions made were lost in the negativity of their conversation. Each person seemed to be in survival mode, trying to protect their position. I guessed that this was their modus operandi in the workplace.

After a little while I intervened and suggested that instead of trying to make contact with the horses, they aim first to simply join the herd passively. They could play the child's game 'Me and my Shadow' each of them with a different horse, remaining at a distance with which the horse was comfortable. They were a little bemused but agreed and went to re-engage with the herd.

Each person slowly took their position about six feet to the side of their chosen horse, moving their feet in time with the front hooves. Hands were generally stuffed in pockets, arms tight to their sides revealing the ongoing stress they all felt. Yet little by little, in the warmth of the morning sunshine they became absorbed in the grazing motion of the horses. I saw their shoulders slowly drop as their minds decompressed and relaxation emanated through their bodies. In time the horses tolerated that their human shadows edged closer and before they knew it each person was miraculously close to a sleek, muscled shoulder beside them. One or two were even stroking the glossy coat of their equine companion.

When we came together after about 20 minutes to explore what had happened I was surrounded by smiling faces. Childlike amazement had replaced the sniping and destructive dialogue. As they talked together it was as if walls had come down around them. One man spoke of how he had forgotten what it was like to feel like himself and couldn't remember the last time he had been so happy. Another spoke of what his colleagues and family had put up with and how he had not even liked himself due to his irritability; the next that some mornings she didn't want to get out of bed to go to work, she was beginning to hate it so much, and often thought about walking out of the office once she got there.

### *Honesty breaks through*

As disclosure invited further confidences the team cast aside their defensive armour and reached a point of stark authenticity. The men and women were seeing each other as friends and allies deserving of support and compassion, not foes who had to be kept at a distance.

The response of the horses to the group on the second day of their programme reflected this shift. They pricked their ears forwards in interested greeting and responded with curiosity and playfulness. They cooperated, enjoyed, trusted and respected the humans they were working with. This positive reinforcement from the horses was further validation for the team of how powerful they could be together. That if they were united and supported each other, not only would their leadership be more effective, life itself could be better if they could be themselves.

Back at the office the week after the programme, everyone was shocked when this same team turned up in casual clothes on the Friday and invited all their colleagues out for a drink at the local pub. It wouldn't be a weekly activity, but it signalled that they would all be trying to bring a human touch to counter the pressures their business was under.

'What have those horses done to you?!' someone exclaimed at the bar, I was told afterwards. 'Are they magic horses or what!' People teased them, but I have no doubt that they liked the new authentic presence, as much as the horses had.

# 26

## *Ruby: A Heart Connection*

### *November 2008*

Being careful not to lose my Wellington boots in the winter mud, I stepped gingerly through the gateway until my feet found solid ground. The 20-acre field yawned before me. I could see seven horses grazing in the near distance. The woman who walked beside me limped, her arthritis was bad.

'I've got to sell them, it's killing me. I can't cope anymore. Especially with winter coming up.' I could tell how hard this decision was for her from the vibration in her voice. She had bred five of the herd from the original two mares she had imported from the United States. They were all traditional American quarter horses. The same breed as Coop.

'I was meant to be breeding them to make a little bit of money. Some hope! I could never bear to let the foals go ...' Her voice trailed off wistfully and she went on, regaling me with her treasured memories until I was shivering with the cold. I wondered if she was delaying the moment when I might agree to buy one of her horses and take them away.

Winston had developed degenerative bone disease in his hind legs – I had been advised that his days as a riding horse were over. So I needed a new friend and, besotted as I had been with Coop, I started searching for someone like him. So here I was, ready to view a 7-year-old mare, the smallest of the herd and advertised at a good price due to having had no training.

At the point when I was feeling that I might need to interrupt my hostess, a pretty bright chestnut horse with a white blaze jumped into a trot and came over to us. She delicately pressed her muzzle into my gloved hands. I melted. I hoped it was her. The woman carried on talking about this and that, oblivious to my need to know.

'Who is this then?' I said casually, trying not to sound too keen.

'Oh, yes, that's her.' she said absentmindedly. 'I thought you realised.'

I was gleeful. Not only because I liked the look of this little horse, but because *she* had chosen *me*. Like Coop had. I called her Ruby because her coat shone red in the sunshine.

Ruby had chosen me that day. But not the life that lay in store for her. Transported to my world, this beautiful horse unravelled, and quickly. All her life she had lived with her mother, her aunt, brothers and sisters. Everything in her new environment frightened her, and she protested explosively. This was not the gentle, sweet mare I had encountered on that chilly day in November. And I couldn't imagine in a million years ever being able to ride her. What on earth had I done?

It didn't take me long to realise that in spite of my horsemanship studies, training and experience I had bitten off more than I could chew. For seven years, Ruby had looked after herself within her herd without much human intervention. She didn't know about dealing with people or learning things from us. Teaching her to accept a rider would be even harder than for a young horse. I had such a lot to learn.

### *Teaching emotional mastery*

On the positive side, Ruby had not been exposed to any mishandling nor desensitised by unsympathetic hands. Conversely this also meant that she picked up on the most subtle changes in my thinking, attitude or emotional response. If I misunderstood her, or felt the mildest frustration, irritation, or impatience, she would fly into a terrified frenzy with all four feet off the ground as she bucked and spun and struggled to get away from me. This in turn would terrify me, and my heightened response would make her even worse. One time, she took fright as I led her past another horse in a field. He charged at her over the fence, teeth bared, protecting his territory. Before I had time to drive him away she was in the air. I thought she would kill me, running round and round me in circles, eyes wild and foaming with sweat across her neck.

Yet, little by little with the help of some talented professionals and lots of studying, Ruby's behaviour made sense to me. And with the kind of feedback she was giving me I was understanding so much more about myself too. She was stretching me to not only a new level of horsemanship but also of emotional awareness and self-management. In particular, I had to be very patient, asking her to learn in incremental steps, never in a hurry and always rewarding the slightest try.

Ruby was also teaching me the need for *absolute* calm, for she would pick up on a mere tremor of apprehension or self-doubt. Because she reacted so quickly and violently to my mistakes, I also had to learn to stay present, even more than I already knew how, to enable me to respond to her in the moment and as intuitively as she did to me. Little by little we got there. It was slow progress because my confidence was easily broken as well as hers. But, eventually, she rewarded my hard work and patience with trust. The heart connection I had experienced with her at that first meeting was recreated. I saw a softening of her demeanour and a peaceful, responsive and gentle partnership evolved which touched me at my core.

Yet still there were times here and there when I would provoke her without knowing what I had done, thought or felt to cause her fright. There was a lot more work still to be done on refining my communication with such a sensitive being. But as I attuned to Ruby and accepted that her responses to me always contained a useful message, she helped me tread the path I had chosen.

## 27

## *Staying On Course*

### *West Norfolk, Summer 2010*

It was one of those days when it felt good to be out on the fens of West Norfolk. There were other times in this flat, monotonous landscape with the easterly wind chilling through to my bones when it did not feel so inspiring. Ruby trotted beneath me, the steady rhythm of her hooves putting up tiny birds from the reeds in the deep drainage ditches alongside the track.

I had moved to West Norfolk to live with my partner. It was the first serious relationship I had been in since my divorce ten years earlier. There were a couple of acres at his home, so we agreed that I would run programmes for small groups of clients or individuals at the rambling farmhouse. The national and global economies had taken a dive and business had suffered so this would keep overheads down. I was balancing that drop in revenue by developing my horse-led therapy practice and offering natural horsemanship instruction. My business partner had gone on to develop a new venture further north so I was working alone now.

Some of my existing corporate clients had already been to work with me and my horses at the farm. Now I had a herd of four – Winston, still the charismatic and bold leader, Ruby and two fluffy palomino miniature Shetland ponies. But it was proving difficult to tempt new clients to make the journey 'out East' where road and rail connections were poor.

### *Old patterns return*

As hard as I tried to stay buoyant I began again to become fretful. Where would the business come from? Would the economy recover? Had I been deluded to think I could make a success of this outlandish idea? My partner was putting me under pressure to get a 'proper job'. Perhaps he was right, and I should stop messing about? My inner critic was back in the driving seat.

As I guided Ruby along the fenland tracks, I was aware that she was more nervy than usual. I tuned into the sensations in my body and noticed those familiar signs of tension had returned: tightness in my jaw, muscles stiff through my lower back and legs, and breath shortened by a taut diaphragm. I was making her as anxious as I was myself. Ah, I recognise this place, this feeling and the thoughts which go with it. I need to take control, and find a way back to positivity.

I asked Ruby to slow into a walk and focussed on being with her, in that moment, rocking with her gait. The thoughts in my head I could return to later, now I needed to be present, for my sake and hers or we would end up in one of the stagnant ditches nearby. I needed to relinquish my concerns for the future as I had learned to do with Coop. With each of her strides I let my breath deepen and my muscles soften. Gradually we both sank into relaxed companionship merging as one with the beauty of nature around us.

### *The herd – holding me to my truth*

My mind was quieter by the time we got home and instead of running indoors to check my e-mails, I sat out in the paddock amongst the herd for a few moments. I allowed myself to soak up the peace the four of them cast around like an invisible, reassuring shadow. I could always see things more clearly when I was here. This was where I could work it all out. It was as if they called me back to myself, back into my body where my spirit could live, instead of getting stuck in my mind where my demons lay.

I thought of the day in Colorado when my wish to share the wisdom of horses with the world materialised. Until that moment I had never really had a strong purpose. I worked hard that was for sure, at school, university, in all my different jobs, in my psychotherapy studies. But I was working hard to 'not fail', rather than to succeed. There was a big difference. And now that I was struggling to win business I had allowed myself to lapse into this old pattern of thinking.

Leaning back on my arms with legs outstretched in front of me I listened to the sound of the horses and ponies tearing at the grass nearby. How I felt in this moment, with them, was the only answer I needed. I didn't have to do anything to win through other than allow myself to have these moments of stillness when I could confidently reconnect with my vision. Then I could stay true to the commitment I had made back in Colorado and continue to allow my path to evolve in the face of the challenges which were presenting. I had to trust I was on course and allow my horses to help me stay there. No compromises. No doubting. The way I was working was uniquely me, with my herd. It was our co-creation.

### *Why not me? Three words to change everything*

The inspiration from my herd would soon be reinforced by a remarkable young woman. If I ever needed a message to

127

transform my wavering conviction into a bold belief that I could succeed, it would be hers. Her words formed into a mantra I would return to time again over the years to come in moments of self-doubt.

The woman, an equestrian Paralympian, was one of the contributors at a natural horsemanship festival where I had been watching some of the most inspiring, relational horsemanship I had ever seen. Astride her elegant, athletic horse she talked eloquently and with harnessed emotion to the crowd seated around the large indoor arena. She told us how, at the age of 22, her back was broken by a falling hay bale and she was left paraplegic. Smashed were her aspirations to become a stunt rider, as she faced life in a wheelchair. She talked about her struggle to come to terms with this change that had been forced upon her. How at first she could not bear to go and see her horses, who lived at the back of her family home, at all. Thinking of a life without riding them again was unbearable.

And then, one day, she felt strong enough to confront her broken dreams and wheeled herself out to the paddock. There was one horse who immediately came to the gate. This was a horse she had started training before the accident using techniques based on relationship, trust, respect and play. The mare looked over the gate as if to say, 'Where have you been?' and 'When are we going to have some fun again?' Bravely she pushed the gate open and wheeled herself through to the other side. Her horse greeted her then stretched down and nuzzled her lifeless legs and she told us how this had made her cry. But then as they reconnected the woman took comfort and courage from this creature who welcomed her so tenderly. The words which had been haunting her for weeks: 'Why me? Why has this happened to me?' were changing. Instead, she thought: 'Why *not* me? Why should I *not* play with my horse again, or even ride?'

'Why should I *not* have some new goals, for the two of us?'

So this extraordinary woman set her sights on becoming a Paralympian. She not only won gold and silver at Beijing in 2008, she also trained her horse herself from her wheelchair rather than turn the mare over to other professionals. Her relationship with her horses remained more important than a medal.

Why not me? Almost a battle cry, rejecting the helpless voice of the victim, and defeating the insidious whispers of 'Are you really good enough?' This woman whose spirit would not be limited either by her body or her negative thinking changed so much with those three words.

## 28

## *Victim No More*

### *I can because ...*

On the first day of their leadership development programme, Geraldine took the lead in disclosing to her fellow participants what she wanted to gain from her learning experience. She talked about building better relationships at work, particularly with key senior people in the organisation. She felt that because she only worked three days a week, she wasn't taken seriously. She didn't necessarily want promotion, with additional responsibility, because of her difficult family circumstances, but she did want to get some of the more exciting and interesting projects that came up. At the moment, they always seemed to go to full-time colleagues.

As Geraldine's work with the horses progressed on the first day, the pattern that quickly emerged was of abandoning what she had set out to do with the horses immediately that things didn't go to plan. She would redefine the task, enlist the help of others, switch horses or even abandon the task completely. I often heard her say the words, 'I can't because ...'

'I can't because the horse is eating ...'

'I can't because this horse doesn't like me ...'

'I can't because there is no point in starting, it will be lunchtime soon ...'

After lunch, Geraldine expressed a desire to work with

the alluring and mischievous Winston. It was not difficult for her to attract his interest and soon he was slipping his nose into the halter. That was when the trouble started. By scratching an itchy spot on his brow vigorously against her shoulder he moved her several paces across the field. I asked whether she was comfortable with what was happening.

'Yes,' she trumpeted, 'Fine! He's saying hello!'

Extending this satisfying game of dominance, Winston forced her to take several steps sideways, this time gently nudging her out of his way with a shoulder.

'And now Geraldine? How are you?'

'Yes, fine!' she replied.

Winston then took matters into his own hands and took Geraldine for a slow but purposeful march around the field, albeit at a gentle and amiable pace. I did not feel that her position was unsafe, but intervened again, enquiring what Geraldine thought was happening.

'Well, I guess he's taken over, hasn't he? He was taking me for a walk rather than the other way round. I was OK with it, but I suppose I should have taken charge. But it felt like fun … well, I think it did anyway.'

'Did it occur to you at any point in the last ten minutes with him that you might want to take leadership?' I explored.

'Hmmm, yes, quite a few times actually,' she giggled. 'I thought I probably looked like a soap on a rope as I followed him around. Or was it a dope on a rope!' But that last comment was tinged with something I couldn't quite put my finger on. Was it disappointment? Resignation? I let silence fall between us for a few moments, choosing not to laugh at the joke she had made against herself, before continuing and asking gently:

'So what stopped you?'

'Well, I just couldn't. He's so huge. It would have been pointless to even try.'

We then revisited what had happened in the morning, and I asked her to reflect on any pattern she felt was emerging.

'Gosh, yes. I see. I often give up before I have even tried doing anything. 'I can't because' is probably the phrase I use most. I get sick of it. Things at home are so difficult, with the kids, my mother with Alzheimer's and of course work ... I rarely get to go out and even when I do I can't have a glass of wine or really relax in case I need to rush over to my parents at the drop of a hat. Dad can't really cope on his own terribly well.'

She fell silent; her eyes became moist.

'What's happening for you, Geraldine?'

'I suppose there's another reason I don't do the things I want to do... because I feel guilty.'

'Guilty ... because ...?'

'Because I wish I didn't have all this to deal with! First it was my father who was ill, now my mother. One of my sons needs regular hospital visits. When am I ever going to get a break? It doesn't seem fair! There! I've said it!' Her voice escalated with anger. 'Sometimes I hate myself because I feel sorry for myself ...not her. I'm so exhausted sometimes and without a life of my own anymore.'

Geraldine released some of the emotion she had long been holding and began the process of shedding the debilitating effect of the self-pity. Over the years her ability to support herself had been eroded and she had come to accept her role as victim. She understood that the martyr's mantle, which she was wearing so well, was crippling her spirit as badly as the difficult domestic issues she faced. It was not really her mother or her son's illnesses that were stealing her life, but those words, 'Why me?' and 'I can't because'.

Geraldine discovered the new energy she could find instead through the words 'Why not me?' as she continued to work with Winston over the next two days. Before long, she took charge of the big charismatic horse who had initially been dominating her, and they were sharing impish yet respectful games. Laughter replaced her self-deprecating humour.

Geraldine wrote to me some time after the programme to share that instead of pushing for more challenging projects she had negotiated a two-day week with her employers so that she could have more time to relax with the family and to invest in herself. She started sailing again, something she had always loved doing, and had found a charity which was able to accommodate her son's medical condition so the whole family were able to take to the water together sometimes. Other times she took valuable time to have more fun by herself. She had stopped saying, 'I can't because' and was now saying, 'I will because I can.' She had chosen to take responsibility for her own happiness.

# 29

## *The Power of Positive Thinking*

### *Disempowered by blame*

Andrew came to work with me a year after the end of a significant relationship. He was still finding it difficult: raking over their old conversations, poring over photographs, and fuming when he saw his ex with his new lover. He said that although he was the first to have been unfaithful, causing a rift in their relationship, he blamed his former partner for the actual break-up.

I asked him what kind of support he had from other people while he was in low spirits, and he talked about such-and-such a friend who never returned his calls, another who was only interested in their new girlfriend these days, and well, the people at work were a waste of space. In Andrew's world, I found that I really couldn't get him to identify anything that was going well.

By the end of the first encounter with the horses, although Andrew had not succeeded in haltering and leading the horses, they had allowed him to approach and stroke them and later on he had even been able to groom one of them. I asked him what he felt had gone well.

'Well, nothing went well really. They pretty much ignored me.'

'Yes, some of the time they did, Andrew. I also saw that as you gained their confidence, there was quite a lot of connection between you and the horses …' I detailed the specifics of what I had seen.

'I suppose there was some good stuff. I still felt disappointed though; I had expected more than that.'

'I'm curious whether there is a tendency to see the negatives in a situation, Andrew, for you right now. It's not unusual that we do that sometimes …'

'You could be right. I guess things have been pretty rubbish lately, so I have become a glass-half-empty person. I've had some bad luck as well and things have been genuinely tough.'

In spite of my best efforts during Andrew's next session he continued to identify himself only with what didn't go well. His energy level diminished gradually, as did my own.

I asked Andrew to write in a journal daily, in the weeks before his next visit, only including the things that had gone well for him and which gave him more energy rather than less. I hoped to find a way of helping Andrew to realise that until he could cease seeing himself as a victim with no responsibility for the situation in which he found himself, it would be difficult to lift himself out of the 'bad luck' he had been having.

The third time he came, we started by reviewing his scribblings. The pages were quite bare to start with but gradually became more populated. We also explored, when things had gone less well, how he had contributed to the situation either by what he had done or by what he had not done.

That day Andrew worked with three of my herd: Winston, and the two diminutive Shetlands Dawn and Ellie. The two ponies would not let him get close at all, but my large and confident gelding allowed Andrew to groom him and put the halter on. When Andrew progressed to leading him around the paddock, however, Winston immediately took charge and dictated what route they took and when he stopped to graze.

When I asked how it had gone, Andrew replied, 'Well it was a bit better – until I started leading. Then it was a disaster. I guess I'm not that good or the horse isn't very well trained.'

### *Empowered by responsibility*

'Regardless of any sense of being 'good' or otherwise, or 'trained' or not, can you share with me what you did or did not do which contributed to creating the situation which arose, Andrew?'

'I couldn't have done much else, could I? I'm not experienced with horses.'

I persisted firmly but gently. 'I didn't ask what else you could have done. I asked how you contributed to creating the situation that arose.'

He fell silent for a moment. I waited.

'Well, I suppose he only took control because I didn't. I suppose I could also have asked for help, but I didn't.'

'And what went well? It wasn't all doom and gloom from where I was standing.'

'The starting bit wasn't too bad I suppose.'

'Say some more about that … and what you did to create success right at the beginning.'

So we continued reviewing what had unfolded and how he had contributed to both the successes and the disappointments.

Andrew came for the fourth time about a month later, and he chose to work with the same trio. He talked animatedly about some things that had gone really well, his social life had improved, and he had even been on a date.

'How are you going to create some success today,

Andrew, and what would success look like for you?'

'Success would look like the herd all responding to me. Not a single horse or pony ignoring me. Maybe lead the ponies somewhere, they wouldn't let me get close last time. And I will create that by believing it can happen. I don't see why I shouldn't really. I made good progress last time.'

He entered the field and approached one of the ponies slowly but positively. She stayed still and let Andrew stroke her, then scratch her shoulder. The other pony walked across, keen to get a scratch too and soon after Winston joined them. The three of them stood respectfully around the man as he ruffled their shaggy manes affectionately. They stayed there together for some time. Andrew then walked away, intending to go and get a halter so he could attempt to lead Dawn or Ellie. But he didn't need the equipment. The ponies followed, ears pricked forwards, matching Andrew's rhythmic pace. Within barely half an hour, he had achieved what he wanted to and more. He had discovered how he could have what he wanted, not by being a victim, but by taking responsibility and believing that good things *could* come from him and to him.

Self-pity and pessimism had been seductive for Andrew. They may have even been useful once, by helping him to attract sympathy from others or even elicit guilt to influence and control them. Being a casualty of circumstance may also have been a convenient way of him avoiding responsibility. The leap he took from this negative frame of mind was not easy but empowered him to create a fresh, happier life.

## 30

## *Committing to Purpose*

One of the mysteries of working with people as they strive for personal or professional growth, is that often I find myself in a parallel learning process with them. Perhaps that is because, sooner or later, our human condition drives us all to grapple with similar questions and events. Or perhaps it is a gift from the universe that I am sometimes able to learn as much from my clients as they from me and my herd.

Amanda sought my help as I was busy applying the 'Why not me?' philosophy to developing my own life. It was a blustery autumn day, and her wavy, wiry, straw-coloured hair was wriggling out of the tightly tied ponytail in the strong breeze as she shared her situation with me.

'Business is good, the team is working well together. I'm happily married with two gorgeous kids who are healthy and happy. I should be satisfied but I notice that I am not. I don't know … I feel like something is holding me back, but I don't know what. All I know is I've been mildly frustrated for a year or more. The business seems to have hit a plateau and we are not getting the new clients or projects we normally would be. I'm also tired most of the time. Ever longer hours, more pressure, less and less time at home with the kids – but with little to show for it. Huh – and I've been piling the weight on. Doesn't seem to matter how strict I am with what I eat.'

In spite of her worries Amanda's effervescent personality shone through. She had a ready smile and I guessed a sense of fun.

'So what would be helpful for you to explore today with me and the horses?' I asked.

'I think the answer is definitely to delegate more to my team so they do more, and I do less. That will free me up to develop new clients and some new service offerings I've got in mind. That is what I should really be doing – not all these operational tasks.'

'So what needs to change for this to happen?' I asked.

'Well, for one, I need to give up on being so controlling. You know, trust people to do what I do as well as I do it. I'm sure they can. I'd like to be less direct in my leadership style too – give them more space to have ideas about new ways of solving old problems. Sometimes I feel I am the only one with the answers, which I suspect limits the team's chances to find their own or new solutions.'

We started working with Ruby, whose vivid chestnut coat was reflected that day in the autumnal scene. Amanda soon created a great rapport with her.

'I would like you to choose what you do next with Ruby.' I handed Amanda a small pack of cards, each one describing optional ways of progressing her relationship with the horse.

After a few moments browsing, Amanda showed me what she had chosen. The card said, 'Run with Horse'. But quickly she put it back saying, 'Perhaps not – I'll do this one, instead.' She had replaced the first task with one that said, 'Walk with Horse.'

She started moving to join Ruby, but I stopped her. 'Hold on, Amanda. Before you continue, tell me a little bit about your first choice and why you changed your mind.'

'Well, I was drawn immediately to running with Ruby. Silly, but I had an image of feeling free and running really fast, my hair blowing in the wind, like in a perfume advert. I'd love to see her move too. Then I thought that sounded a bit daunting, so I chose something safer. Something more within my reach. So I chose walking not running.'

I challenged her gently. 'OK, so I would like you to do what you really want to do. I think that is running.'

She was up for it. 'OK – you're on!'

### *Run with the horse*

She turned back to Ruby and spent a while connecting with her again, speaking as if to a child, 'Now, we're going to run, aren't we, will that be OK?'

Then she commenced leading the horse away in a gentle walk. Ruby followed willingly but when Amanda skipped into a jog she carried on walking at the same slow pace. Amanda added more verbal cajoling and waved her arms to encourage her companion to run. Soon, she was running furiously on the spot alongside the ambling horse who then halted abruptly.

'Guess that didn't work very well! I was running like mad, but the horse wasn't! Do I get five out of ten?' Amanda's defeated smile faded into resignation.

I inquired what might be familiar about what had happened.

'Well, it feels like it does at work. My legs go faster and faster, I work harder and harder, and I still don't get anywhere. In the end, I am doing a marathon but everything around me is staying the same. I end up running to stand still, that is how my life feels most of the time.'

'What do you change in order to not stand still? Try again with Ruby, asking yourself that question.'

Amanda went back to the patient mare and encouraged her a couple more times, and although Ruby walked faster, she still didn't want to run.

'Oh, I can't be bothered with this! I knew I should have

picked the other card, then we could have all gone for our tea break by now!'

'Before we take a break, talk to me about something you are really passionate about; talk to me about your dreams.'

Amanda talked with verve about an expedition to Alaska she was planning for her father's 70th birthday, whale watching and salmon fishing.

'And what will this trip mean to you both?'

'It's something he has always hankered after. One or other of us has always been too busy. But he had a cancer scare last year, so I made my mind up that I would take him – just Dad and me because Mum and my husband don't like being on water. We have not been away together, the two of us, since he took me camping when I was 18, when we climbed Scafell.'

As she talked, she became more animated and seemed to grow 2 inches in height. Even her hair seemed to get bigger.

'And what has it taken to get this trip organised after so many years?'

She pondered. 'Well, apart from the obvious planning, not much really, once we had made the commitment to do it.'

'OK, so can you find the same kind of commitment for your run with the horse?'

Amanda looked amused. 'Ah, I get it. Yes OK. I will have a go.'

### Committing with the whole self

The woman rested her hand on the horse's neck for a moment. Then fixing her gaze on a point across the field, she took a deep breath and stepped forwards briskly. She was holding her body upright but looked relaxed. The horse followed her instantly and willingly. Within ten or twelve paces, Amanda jumped into a run with her head high and chin in the air, and miraculously her four-legged companion followed suit. Ruby stayed at Amanda's shoulder as she jogged, ready to go or slow as she asked.

And as they ran and walked intermittently around the field, the horse's ears flicked back and forth her attention staying with Amanda every step of the way. Amanda's expression was gleeful. At first, she ran because it had been a task she had set out to do, but now it looked like she was running because it felt good.

'Way-hay!' Amanda shouted as they turned in a loop at the bottom of the field. The two of them were heading back towards me when Ruby erupted into a canter. Amanda couldn't keep up and doubled over breathless with hands on her thighs. The horse slid to a stop ahead of her.

We sat down to debrief.

'Wow, now I get it!' she shared after a few minutes reflecting and writing in her journal. 'I've always worked really hard to get people to follow me as a leader, and have always nurtured the belief that they might not. So I have always been looking backwards effectively, rather than trusting that my energy and vision will inspire people to follow. And because I have been afraid they won't follow me, I have not been able to fully commit to my vision and my direction. It is this which slows me down in growing the business. I'm not sure now it is anything to do with delegation.'

Running in the field with the horse, Amanda had found the courage to do what she didn't think she could. But more than that, she had realised that finding the courage and setting the goal was not enough on its own. To make it happen, she had to *commit* her whole self to what she wanted to do.

### *Intention is not enough*

Amanda learned that mentally setting herself a goal and intending to do something was not enough. If she was going to spend more time with her children, or grow the business, or empower her team more, she had to commit to that intention without hesitation and in a purposeful way. She wrote to me some months later. As well as making changes at work she had also made a commitment to take up running; something she had always secretly wanted to do but had never found the courage. She was training for a 10k run and was aiming for a half-marathon.

Witnessing the success of Amanda reminded me of the importance of unshakeable commitment in creating the future that I wanted. Little did I realise that around the corner I would need every fibre of strength I could muster.

# 31

## *Gordon*

**January 2012**

Embraced by the delicious mattress beneath me I pulled the warm duvet around my neck. It had been an arduous drive from West Norfolk to Hampshire where I was staying at my friend Sarah's house. I was attending an appointment the next day with an organisation based not too far from her home and needed to get a good night's rest. That might be difficult because I was excited. I knew the meeting could lead to a project big enough to take my business, and with it the acceptance of horses as valid contributors to human development, to the next level.

My dog sitter had let me down at the last minute so Milo and Holly, my now elderly Jack Russells, were down at the side of my bed in Sarah's guest room. Sleep enveloped me quickly in spite of their faint snoring and yipping as they dreamed of chasing rabbits.

From deep in my sleep I heard my phone ringing. By the time I had dragged myself into semi-consciousness and got my bearings I had missed the call. I squinted at the illuminated screen and saw that it had been Kate, my eldest brother Gordon's wife. I knew something had to be wrong. It was just before midnight.

It must be Lorenz, my stepfather. He was 90 years old and quite frail. It wouldn't be a surprise. I put the light on and called her back. The tight voice that answered, I barely recognised.

'It's Gord. He's in hospital,' she blurted. 'They don't know if he will make it through the night.'

Gordon, my older brother. 52 years old. Not Lorenz. I couldn't get my head round this.

Hurriedly Kate explained how he had been taken ill with flu-like symptoms two days earlier, and then that evening she had noticed a purple rash forming on the tips of his earlobes and nose. She called the ambulance fearing meningitis. In fact, he had sepsis and by the time he got to hospital his condition was already critical.

'I'm coming. Should take me three or four hours maybe to get there.' I breathed deeply, suppressing the urge to vomit, as my skin became cold with the shock. I had to gather myself. It took me less than ten minutes to dress, load us all into the car and hug Sarah as she handed me some food and a flask of hot coffee for the journey.

At half past midnight, I set off into the night daring not to contemplate the gravity of the situation I faced. I couldn't afford to fall apart; I had to stay calm and drive safely. At least the roads were dry and the sky was clear. The presence of the freight wagons, some lit up like Christmas trees, was comforting and brought an inappropriate air of festivity as they swept along the highway.

Kate met me, pallid and drawn, in the hospital car park and escorted me to Gordon's bedside in the emergency ward. It was 4am. He was conscious but distressed and surrounded by doctors. His breathing was laboured, and he was already wired up with multiple drips and tubes in both arms and hands. It was shocking. He looked at me with his piercing blue eyes and attempted a smile. For a moment, he was still.

'Alright, Pammie. What the hell are *you* doing here?' That was such a typical thing for Gord to say.

'Just passing, Gord,' I replied, in the casual way too that

he might have expected from me. Ours had never been an emotional relationship, however fond.

Then he rolled away from me trying, in vain, to turn onto his side. 'I can't get comfy. I feel so shit, I think I'm going to die,' he said. My stomach shrank in panic.

'Don't be daft,' said Kate, kissing him and stroking his brow. 'You're in good hands, they are getting antibiotics into you, you'll start feeling better soon.'

We stayed an hour or so until the doctor suggested that we left to get some rest so that they could take Gordon up onto the critical care ward, he would need to be ventilated and to start a blood transfusion. His breathing was increasingly laboured as the purple rash extended its sprawling fingers across his face, chest, arms and hands. Back at their house I lay down on the bed. I couldn't find sleep. When we returned to the hospital a few hours later, Gordon was unconscious. It was easier to be with him than before.

This, now, was the time to be brave. My nephews, young men in their early twenties who should not have had to see their father like this, had arrived. And Gordon's best friend and his wife had come too. All of us connected in the horror of this tragedy unfolding. My fists clenched tight and my whole body braced, I muttered: 'Please don't let him die' and 'I can do this. I can be strong.'

The following 48 hours blurred one into the next as the medical team waged a monumental battle to save my brother. We took rest when we could and comfort from each other when we couldn't, clinging to the hope that next time, the hourly blood test would indicate that his body was beginning to fight the infection. It never did. His immune defences were overwhelmed. By Friday evening, our hopes died as we watched his ravaged body drift further and further from us. At six minutes past six on the Saturday morning, the mesmerising pulse of the monitor all of a sudden slowed and, before I was ready, it stopped.

## *A spiritual awakening*

Then, as I gazed down on my brother's body lying unrecognisable on the bed, I had a sense of him, and of his vibration, filling the room. His physical form was lifeless there in front of me. But he had not gone, in fact he was all around. It was as if the air vibrated to the frequency of his laugh, his smell, his look, his way of being. It was like the time when my mother died, and I was woken by that powerful sense of her surrounding and embracing me as she came to say goodbye.

That memory of being so close to Mum, of sensing her powerful love and spirit, had never left me. A part of me always wondered if this encounter was the product of my disturbed mind, distraught from the distress of watching her die. For a long time, I felt unable to share my experience in case people thought I was crazy. Other times I held it close and, when I missed her the most, I could conjure that same feeling of her arms around me, of her scent and her presence, for comfort and strength.

But this time I could not be mistaken. I had been awake, conscious and present to witness what happened. It wasn't something to see, or even feel. It was stranger than that. It was something to sense.

I had experienced the separation of form and formless. I knew now what was meant by spirit. That the essence of each of us is not about our body, or what we perform or achieve in that body, about what we have or what we do. Our spirit, our essence, is about being. It is the life that pulses and ripples within us. It is what is left when the heart beats no more. It is something that is sensed, and something of the senses. It is something which resonates, which vibrates. It is a silent music, and the emotions and feelings that animate us during life are the notes, the chords and the crescendos of that symphony.

This revelation was Gordon's gift to me.

We all cried and held each other around the bed and bade him our last excruciating farewells. I hoped that in spite of him having been unconscious he had heard us all talking in the days and hours before he passed away, reminiscing about the crazy things we'd done and the memories we treasured. I hoped that he died knowing how deeply he was loved.

We left the hospital at dawn. I was numb, exhausted, bewildered. There had been a heavy frost, and I was grateful for the biting chill and brightness of the breaking day after the darkness we had been living. It helped me feel alive and reminded me that the world was still beautiful. And that my brother's spirit lived on.

*32*

## *Finding Joy Amongst Grief*

### *The brother I had*

Gord had not always been the big brother I'd have chosen.
He had never looked after me, helped me out or as a teenager
fixed me up with any of his friends. He was quirky, eccentric,
irritable and irritating. Yet he was also lovable and very, very
funny. Irreverently so. As a child, he had been the master of
play and the creator of elaborate make-believe games – my
younger brother Colin and I were his devoted followers. As
pre-school gangsters named Mr and Mrs Moustache (spelt
Mastash) we staged heists at the bank while our mother was
at the counter, or later, we graduated to operating as private
detectives and staked out our neighbours' houses to detect
any suspicious goings-on.

Gordon was unusually clever in a brilliant kind of way
that even his teachers and lecturers didn't get, and I certainly
didn't. After he died, we found carefully-compiled
notebooks listing and reviewing every book he had read,
every beer recipe he had developed, used and tested, and
every electronic invention he had created (including a bat
detector and a fridge alarm). His copy of Stephen Hawking's
*A Brief History of Time* was annotated in the margins with
Gordon's own theories and commentary on his views on the
work. Most touching were the dozens of beautiful
watercolour drawings he had painted, stacked secretly in his
office, and never shared with the world.

If I had fully understood my brother, I wonder if our relationship might have been different. If we might have found a way of being more easy together. I knew he loved me, but it was hard for him to say or show it. At least in a way that made sense to me. Perhaps the lectures on some complicated scientific theory, and the urgent need to impart information to me about the freezing temperatures of particular gases, the galactic path of a particular star, or the life-cycle of a desert badger, was his way of saying that he cared. He would trap me in a corner of the kitchen then pour out the information – I would end up laughing, or escaping, and he would implore, 'Pammie! You really need to listen to me! You need to know this! It's a life or death thing!'

But now he was gone. He had been woven into the fabric of my lifetime. We shared precious memories of innocence, and he connected me with my parents who had already died. I was shocked at how keenly I felt his loss. In society's hierarchy of bereavement, if there is one, I felt that the loss of a sibling wasn't really up there. When my parents had died, particularly my mum, condolences, flowers, cards and good wishes came in abundance. It really helped. Losing Gordon, a brother, I could count the cards that I received on one hand. The world preferred not to mention what had happened. 'Were you close?' some people would ask. And what did I say to that? 'No, not really.' Because we weren't close in the way that people would understand that word to mean.

And yet losing him seemed much harder than my parents. He had been the only other person surviving who had been around all my life. And he was so young. Barely older than me. It seemed outrageous, unbelievable. How could it be possible that a healthy man dies, in days, in the 21$^{st}$ century? Frankly, it was terrifying. If he could go so quickly, so unexpectedly, then so could I.

### *It is good to be alive*

During the weeks following Gord's death, life became about getting by. No longer could I start each day by bouncing out of bed saying, 'It's a wonderful day!' because each day was full of pain. Working on my own became hard and lonely.

But what I could say to myself and absolutely mean it, was:

'Today, it's wonderful to be alive. This moment, it's good to be here, however I feel.'

By endeavouring to be present in each moment as it passed I was becoming grateful for my life and health in a new way and I found that there was joy to be had even in my grief. On a frosty morning as the rising sun blessed my morning walk with the dogs, on a cosy afternoon baking cakes with my partner's children or each time I inhaled the comforting smell of my horses' warm winter coats as I groomed them, I was able to find peace.

Now I had lost my mum, dad and oldest brother, not to mention my stepson those years earlier. My younger brother lived abroad and I saw him seldom. But my grief was different to before. I could stay connected with the whole woman I had become, instead of becoming the orphaned child who used to beckon in darker days.

## 33

## *Courage to Grieve*

It was a year or so after my brother died when Frankie sat in front of me, placing both hands flat on the table in front of her.

'What I need is to rekindle some enthusiasm for my business – I'm a freelance editor – and develop some new ideas for growing my client base. And get excited by it all again. I've always loved what I do – I don't know what is wrong with me these days – guess I have lost my mojo! Maybe it's my age, a mid-life crisis or something.' She rolled her eyes comically.

It was not humour though that I saw in her eyes – grief had become a familiar emotion for me, and I recognised it straight away.

'OK – tell you what then. Let's start at the beginning and talk a bit about how life was before you lost your mojo.'

Frankie's words were controlled initially but soon tumbled as she told her tragic story. She had lost her husband five years earlier in his early forties after fifteen years of happy marriage.

'You know – people talk about soul mates, but we really were. There weren't many places we didn't go trekking together with our two beloved collies. Together all the time, happy pretty much most of the time. I lost my best friend as well as my husband and my lover.' Her eyes brimmed and for a moment I thought they might spill. But she briskly wiped them away and smoothed her hair back from her face.

'But I haven't come to talk about all that. I've done the bereavement counselling bit. I'm here to work on my motivation. I don't think all that has much to do with losing Bill. Sure, I miss him, but I cope with it quite well and am getting on with my life. In fact, it's weird because after Bill died I had a surge of motivation – that was when I was best at my job. I had the most successful year financially. Full of ideas, new clients, always busy. I seemed to be fearless too. I suppose I felt I had nothing left to lose.'

'So, tell me more about what it means to you, losing motivation?' I invited.

'The business has stopped coming in and I can't really be bothered to do anything about it. Then I get gripped with worry about whether I will survive or not. Perhaps I have been doing the wrong job all these years. But if that IS true what the hell am I going to do now, in my forties?' Her shoulders were high and tense, and her face was pale. Every part of her was invested in containing her emotion.

Frankie wrung her hands together and stared over my shoulder and through the open door behind me to the two horses who were grazing in the paddock. Her eyes became moist again and she lapsed into silence.

'What's happening, Frankie?' I asked gently.

'I was thinking that I would never have felt like this with Bill around. We were always having jokes, planning a trip or recovering from one. Life was exciting. I never felt alone ... like I do now.'

And then the tears came, softly. And as she released herself into her grief, I heard the horses, who were maybe 30 feet behind me, blow out and snort, again and again. This was a sign that they, too, were relaxing. Even out there in the field, through the open doors of the classroom, they could feel her relief as she allowed her sorrow to flow.

Frankie reached for some tissues and blew her nose.

'God I feel stupid now. It was five years ago. But it still feels so real. The trouble is it feels like ancient history to most people. No one ever wants to talk about him or what I am going through any more. Not even my parents. His parents liked to chat about him, but I don't see them very often. The world expects me to be over it, cured. Especially now I have a new partner, people look at me and think – oh, she's OK now. But I don't know if I will ever get over it. The time in the hospital those last few days ...' Her voice trailed away. I could only imagine how distressing it would have been for her to lose a soulmate, a spouse, in the way that she had. We sat together in solemn silence for a little while. Then as her breathing began returning to normal, I asked gently:

'It feels like a good time to go and see the horses, Frankie, would that be OK for you?'

### *No words needed*

Frankie had owned a pony as a child so felt comfortable around them and after hovering for a short while went to sit in the sun on the grass near the small herd. One of the mares, Autumn, looked up and with deliberate yet mellow pace arrived beside the woman. The dark brown horse with a tumble of black mane dropped her head and brushed across Frankie's hair with her lips. Frankie stretched a hand up, stroking the strong muscled neck as it stooped, then stood so she could lay her cheek against the horse's mane. I saw Autumn breathe deeply, simultaneously to Frankie's shoulders dropping as she too exhaled. They stood together for a while. No words were needed. Frankie's grief was acknowledged and witnessed.

After a while, the horse slowly moved away, and Frankie faced me. Her eyes were less watery, and brighter. There was colour in her cheeks although they were also streaked and puffy from crying.

'Perhaps it isn't my motivation I need to address after all,' she said, resigned.

Over the following year, Frankie was able to revisit the loss of her husband, and around the horses it was easier to shed the tears she had been holding onto for so long. Her feelings of grief had become frozen inside her, and she was only now strong enough to bring them out into the open again. With the horses, she could do so without needing to use words which only served to re-traumatise her. She could feel supported with their steady, comforting presence and honour her emotions. No one was judging her, or reinforcing the sense that 'she should have got over it by now'. It had taken five years for Frankie to build enough strength to grieve. By that point, she had become exhausted by the effort of soldiering on. And while pain filled her world there was no space for lightness, creativity or enthusiasm any more. It was no wonder that she found it hard to promote her business.

### *Allowing the pain to live*

When Frankie was able to allow her grief to live and breathe it was able to move through and out of her body instead of being a heavy weight inside. Then she found that little by little she could begin to let it go, so there became space for other things, for new plans, new ideas, new hopes. She found that she was able to revive the many happy memories that had been obscured by the distress of her husband's illness and to connect more strongly with the love that they had once shared.

### *Happiness is not about the destination*

Frankie carried on working with me for a year or more, visiting every month or talking on the phone if she could not make the journey. Devastation was slowly replaced by a sorrowful peace and later her innately adventurous spirit returned. The part of her which had died as her husband's health deteriorated was flourishing once again.

Still raw from the loss of my brother, Frankie's courage inspired me without her knowing it at the time, although I shared that with her later. She reaffirmed for me that whilst bereavement can be immeasurably painful it can also bring us riches and depth. That at the end of the day you cannot control what happens in your life. You can only choose how you respond to what happens. Loss teaches you that happiness is not about the destination of your journey; it is about how able you are to find joy amongst the pain, along the way.

## 34

# *Horses: Our Spiritual Guides*

## *West Norfolk, January 2012*

### *Making sense of spirit*

No-one else had arrived to feed their horses when I reached the livery yard where I kept Winston and Ruby during the winter months. It was my first morning back since leaving home more than a fortnight earlier for a two-day business trip which turned into a three-week ordeal, having stayed in Cheshire to help organise Gordon's funeral. Anxious to be reunited with my horses I had woken sooner than I should have, given how exhausted I was. It was early and still dark.

I closed the car door, and heard Ruby and Winston in greeting. They couldn't see me out in the car park which was situated behind the stables but knew the sound of my vehicle. Their call snatched back the part of me which was still in the hospital, replaying the awful events in the edges of my mind. It still all seemed so incredible, what had happened, but no, it was true. The sick feeling in my stomach told me that.

Amongst the emotional carnage, something else had been growing in my consciousness over the days since he died. It felt important. This was my encounter with Gordon's spirit as it left his physical body. The experience was helping me to make sense of so much else. I was redefining my understanding of 'spirit'. It was more tangible than I had ever thought, like pure life-force, manifesting something universal, powerful, beautiful.

But what did it really mean? Was it possible to sense the essence of a human, or indeed a horse, in the normal course of events? Experiencing them as a spiritual entity, a vibration of life-force, rather than as a 'thing'? Could we see others in a multi-dimensional way encompassing their form and formlessness? Was this meeting with Gordon's spirit showing me a different way of perceiving life itself?

I stepped onto the path which took me into the quadrangle of the stable yard and the horses were there filling my view, so large and full of life. Hmm, I wondered ... could they help me to find some of the answers I was looking for? And could this lead me to another clue as to how I could communicate better with them?

## *A different way of perceiving*

I knew already that my horses honoured me, and other humans, by seeing our essence rather than simply our physical form – that was what my work with clients was based upon. Now, had I finally understood how to reciprocate this when I was with them? Could I stop seeing them as 'a horse' and start experiencing each horse as a spiritual being, with its own presence and energy?

As well as their ten hungry stable mates, Ruby and Winston were stretching their necks over their doors in greeting or perhaps eager anticipation of their breakfast. I approached Ruby first and instead of walking right up to her as I normally would I stood several feet away and took a moment to find stillness. I created a soft focus through my eyes, relaxing them, and being conscious not to *see* her, but to *sense* her. Not to look at the edge of her body, her skin and fur, as where she ended but rather as where she might begin. Not seeing her as a horse, a creature, a thing, but trying to tune into her vibration.

As I did so, she lowered her head gently, a sign of relaxation. Then she yawned, stretched her lips and blinked slowly, letting out a sigh – all clear signs of calmness and comprehension. This was unusual when she was waiting to be fed after a long night in a cold stable!

'Hmmm, interesting!' I thought. 'Let's try another.'

I approached Winston with the same filter on my vision. And he responded in a similar way. Curious as to whether this was because I knew my own horses well, I then approached every horse stabled around the yard, who all belonged to other people and with whom I rarely interacted. The results were identical. Perceiving the horses in this way felt different for them, that was clear. I guessed that they liked it and felt comfortable. I imagined them thinking, 'At last! She gets it!'

It felt different for me too. Paradoxically, I felt that by not 'seeing' them, I had succeeded in allowing them to be seen. That I had connected with them in a way I had not before. For me, my gut, which was still tight with grief, softened. I could breathe deeper. I felt that I had understood something profound about what makes each of us, and each creature, uniquely who we are, and how the sanctity of life dances within us. How easily, I thought, can we overlook the true essence of ourselves, and of others, as it beats deeply in our souls.

I thought of all the times I had unwittingly upset Ruby. How it must have been for her to not be fully seen. How, instead of engaging with her essence, I was operating within a 'cause and effect' model of horse and human behaviour: I do 'x' so she does 'y'. How clumsy, how primitive that seemed.

What did these insights mean, then, for my work as well as for my relationships with my herd? Perhaps what the horses were helping people with wasn't about their emotional and relational difficulties, or being better leaders and team members. Those could be outcomes of a successful intervention but was there something much more fundamental going on? Were the horses, by perceiving us in all of our dimensions and inviting us to do the same, really our spiritual guides, leading us to a place of truly knowing ourselves and our place in the world?

### *Spirituality: 'The S-word'*

This nascent belief slowly took shape for me, yet I could not conceive of discussing it with anyone. Not yet. Talking about spirituality felt risky, particularly in an organisational setting. In some contexts it could antagonise, other times estrange, and lead to being labelled variously religious, hippy, wacky or airy-fairy. Spirituality, the 'S-word', was avoided in conversation to prevent offence, like politics or religion. Elsewhere I knew such matters to be perfectly commonplace and the lifeblood of day-to-day existence or alternatively the subject of rigorous intellectual and academic analysis. I was aware, too, of the deeply personal nature of spiritual experience and belief. Was it not true that I had come to my new awareness at one of the most vulnerable and distressing moments of my life? I didn't know if I could share it with anyone. Perhaps there lies the reason why many of us struggle to share a collective understanding of what it is to be a spiritual creature. It is simply too private, and maybe too painful.

It felt like confusing territory. But for horses it seemed straightforward. Perhaps it could be for me too? As Gordon passed away, I couldn't see his spirit, but what I sensed all around me was nonetheless palpable. It was his essence. It wasn't complicated at all. When I opened my heart and closed my seeing eyes to my horses, they responded by connecting peacefully with me and I with them. We encountered the essence of each other. That too felt simple. And beautiful. Far from being an ephemeral, mystical or religious experience, it was something which in its purest form came from nature.

## 35

## *Being with What Is*

Although explicitly addressing concepts of spirituality was challenging, I was discovering that, actually, it wasn't always necessary in order for my own insights to help me support my clients in pragmatic ways.

Simon was a senior leader in a large manufacturing business. For him a spade was definitely a spade and in his own words 'he took no prisoners'. He sat with his team in front of me at the beginning of their 2-day team development programme. He had worked hard all his professional life and put in the hours, he said. It was a tough industry, and it wasn't getting any easier to turn a profit. He had been living on adrenalin longer than he could remember. I didn't need him to tell me that, the tension around his eyes, mouth and jaw told that particular story well.

### *Searching for balance*

'I know we're here to work on team issues, but personally I'd like to learn a bit more about how I can achieve a better balance in my life. I had a health scare a couple of years ago, a heart attack. It frightened me. I know I need to work less and relax more. But I don't seem able to manage it. The company have sent me on training courses to help me delegate, so I would work less hours. I've been doing lots of things in my own time too. I'm not the sort of person to do things by halves, I work hard at anything I put my mind to.

Changed my diet, joined a gym, read books, been on workshops, even joined a meditation group although I don't often get to go to be honest. But still nothing seems to be changing; I'm still stressed and flogging myself half to death. It is SO frustrating.'

A short time later we all stepped out into the field and Simon asked to go in to meet the horses first. Unsurprisingly, given the tension he was holding, Ruby kept walking away, slowly, but with determination. There was no way she was letting him close. He shared his frustration with me and the rest of his team and tried again to approach her. There was still no change. The pattern continued throughout that first day both with Ruby and the other horses he attempted to meet. His perseverance was unequalled and, in spite of being disappointed, he stayed open to learning and took on board the coaching and guidance he received. Still none of the horses or ponies connected with him. We sat to debrief at the end of the day. He was understandably deflated and exhausted.

'I don't know what I need to do to get them to let me close. I've tried everything.' Alongside the excitement of his colleagues who had built some good relationships with the herd his voice sounded all the more hopeless.

'I can't believe how patient you've been, Simon,' one of his colleagues offered. 'Well done. I'm really proud of you.'

Simon's eyes filled up. 'I guess it feels the same as at work. I always try so hard – even at relaxing – but nothing changes. I'm still the irritable so-and-so who is hardly ever home. Who snaps at my team, and my family.'

And then with real emotion, he said, 'I might have looked patient out there today, but I didn't feel it. I really wanted to shout and scream at those horses. It was excruciating to persevere and still not get them to do what I wanted. It's like when my new grandson comes to visit. He is the first grandkid in the family – he starts crying – it's not his fault, but I can't bear it. I can't say that, of course, my daughter would be gutted. So I leave the room. The worst of it is I remember when she was growing up it was the same, but I wasn't always able to control it. I have shouted at her, and at my wife, more often than I like to admit. I'm not proud of that.'

The group fell silent. Everyone was moved at the level of disclosure, and how much he wanted to change.

### *I want to be myself*

The next morning, the group returned, and Simon chose to work with Ruby again.

'I need to finish this,' he said.

'And how will you be different to yesterday?' I asked.

'I'm going to let go of my expectations. Actually stop trying so hard. In fact, I'm not going to try at all. I'm exhausted with trying. I didn't sleep much last night with all this going on in my head. I really don't want to feel like this anymore – frustrated, stressed and putting so much pressure on myself.'

Simon's words were poignant, describing how he had lost himself, and smothered his spirit, in his need to achieve.

Simon then went into the paddock where Ruby was grazing, took his coat off, put it waterproof side down on the wet grass and dropped down on it. He turned away from the horse and gazed out across the landscape that rolled away into the horizon, where the hilltop trees were turning to springtime shades of lime green and soft grey. Two hares raced across the slope opposite, and the cry of a circling buzzard pierced the silence. Five minutes passed, then ten, and nothing happened. Then fifteen … still nothing. Ruby continued grazing a good distance away. But then she peered across at him as if she had only just noticed that there was someone there. She paused, then ambled over. He stood up slowly, ready to greet her. She nuzzled his outstretched hands and then came up close, sniffing his clothing. He stroked her purposefully and she stayed, enjoying it. His face shone with pleasure. They stood together, becoming acquainted, until I had to signal silently to Simon that we had to finish off. He gently patted the horse and turned to walk away. To his amazement, she followed at his shoulder all the way to the gate. At first, he tried to conceal his delight and looked bashful. Then his jubilation broke through, and he punched the air, 'Yes! I did it!' Then turning to the rest of the team who were observing in respectful silence, he placed his hand on Ruby's neck and said, 'Meet my new best mate.'

### *Stop working, start being*

The rest of the day saw a harmonious and playful relationship develop between the man and the chestnut mare. She followed him at a walk, sometimes accompanied by his team mates, through an obstacle course built from poles and traffic cones. She stopped when he stopped and moved when he moved. He groomed her and picked her feet up. As he played with the horse, it seemed like Simon was transforming before my eyes. The lines were falling away from his face, and he was looking younger, taller, more vivid. Everything he did with the horse seemed effortless. Most experienced horsemen could not have built the rapport that he did with this horse in less than a day.

As we closed the programme, he was asked what he would be taking away from his experience. He replied, 'I need to stop working so hard. I have to let go ... and just be me. It is that simple. Ruby reminded me of that. I also have to stop trying to make everything so perfect. Stop worrying about the things that don't matter and pay attention to the things that do matter – like my relationships, like my health.'

A year later, I received an email from Simon on the anniversary of the programme. 'My family and my team still say I am a changed man. No more shouting, no more stress. Give Ruby a big hug from me.'

### *Letting go to let spirit be*

Simon had let go of something elemental on that day in the field, I couldn't be sure what it was, and indeed he may not have been either. That didn't matter, what counted was that it had helped him to realise something that none of his reading, training courses or striving had done – how to allow his cheerful, joyful spirit to emerge. That is what had engaged Ruby so quickly. And having experienced those precious moments with the gentle mare when he allowed himself to be with what is, instead of relentlessly pursuing something better, he would always know how to return to that state when he needed to.

# 36

## *Spirit as Guide*

Alongside grieving for my lost brother I treasured the lesson I had learned at his hospital bedside. It continued to ripple gently through my interactions with everyone around me. I came to know myself differently – as that which my body contains, not that which my body represents. I noticed that by learning to recognise my own unique essence and vitality in this way, my awareness of what was good for me, and not, what helped my spirit to thrive, or inhibited it, became more and more finely tuned. Being with the horses in whatever capacity was like plugging myself into a universal power-socket, leaving me peaceful, energised and trusting of whatever path lay ahead for me. I gave myself permission to spend as much time with them as I could. When Gail came to work with me and began talking about the reasons which had caused her to seek some support, it was immediately apparent to me that she could benefit in the same way from some time with the herd.

### Serial betrayal

Gail had been with her partner for 12 years and had discovered the previous year that, not for the first time, he had been having a relationship with another woman. She had accepted his regretful promises of future fidelity and they had made another 'fresh start'. But this time it didn't feel fresh for her; in fact, it felt jaded. She was tired of it.

'But that's not why I have come,' she said, 'I'm here because I don't seem to be able to sleep and am exhausted all the time.'

As we walked down to where the horses were grazing Gail chatted about her own horse.

'I haven't ridden for ages though,' she said. 'I lost my confidence a while ago. So now I have an expensive pet!' Behind her smile were shades of wistful sadness. 'I've loved riding since I was a kid, I miss it to be honest. Perhaps you can help me with that as well.'

As we worked with the horses during that first meeting, I became curious about the way in which Gail paid constant attention to what the horses were feeling. Whenever I asked her how *she* was doing, her response would be about them. 'Well, he seems tense,' or 'I don't think he likes me, I'll give him more space.'

I played this observation back to her.

'I really appreciate your care and respect for the horses Gail. I am also interested in how *you* are doing right now. To which she responded, 'Oh, me? I'm fine!'

'Could you say some more about what 'fine' means to you, Gail?'

'Well, you know, I'm OK.'

I persisted. 'And could you say some more about what OK means to you? How that is to be OK?'

'Well, I suppose, honestly, I don't think I'm doing that well. I feel like a failure – I have a horse for heaven's sake, I should be able to get yours to cooperate with me. But they won't even lift their heads to look at me. But I'm OK with that. I don't think I have much right to come in here and start asking them to do stuff while they are eating. I don't blame them really.'

'Hmmm. That doesn't sound fine – now that you put it like that, Gail.'

The woman fell silent and I could see her eyes filling up under the shock of brown hair which had fallen out of her pony tail. 'No, I suppose it isn't. But I've got used to feeling this way. Like a failure. Like I'm not worth any attention. Worrying all the time about upsetting people. I don't really know what has happened to the woman I used to be. That woman – you know – I used to like her. I don't like this person I have become. Always whining, always hesitating, always crying ...'

Over the course of the next six months, Gail returned every four weeks to spend time with us. Initially, the work was about simply learning to be still and present so that she could relax into the nurturing energy of the herd. Then we explored how she might understand and satisfy her own needs as well as those of my horses. Her soul was recharging not only when she was with us, but also with her own horse as she learned to relate to him in a new way.

As her spirit grew in strength it was evident to Gail how badly she had neglected to nurture it. How willing she had been to settle for second best and compromise so vastly on what she needed to be happy. What filtered through was that it wasn't only with respect to her riding that she had lost self-assurance, it was in all areas of her life. But how could she believe in a stranger? Because that was what she had become to herself in her efforts to keep her partner. She thought she had tolerated his behaviour out of love, but as her sense of her true value grew she realised that she did it out of fear of being rejected.

### *Spirit to decide*

But perhaps the most significant shift for Gail, which helped her make the life changes she needed, was grasping that it was her responsibility and no other's to cherish and nourish her essential self. Yes, she should be able to expect that from her partner too. But first it had to come from her. By placing the well-being of her spirit at the centre of her decision-making Gail had the only compass she needed to navigate her way to self-love and fulfilment. She could no longer tolerate deception and betrayal in her relationship and how it diminished her. When they separated she discovered that leaving her partner was hard, but not as hard as it had been living with him. In time Gail bought her own house and absorbed herself in creating a home in which she could start a new life. She rediscovered a creative energy for interior design and furnishing which would later even give birth to a new business venture. Moving away from what was detrimental to her spirit and towards what brought her pleasure guided her towards these life-changing decisions. She told me that she was lonely at times but was able to spend more time with her horse, rebuilding their relationship. And little by little, Gail rediscovered the woman that she had always been, the one she liked.

### *Freed from the need to please*

Gail's vitality had been smothered by her need to please someone else. She was already aware of this pattern when she came to work with me, and told me that it stemmed from attachment difficulties in childhood. But knowing this cognitively was not enough to stop turning herself inside out to gain approval. With the horses she finally rekindled how it *felt* to be herself and to be accepted for who and what she was. She appreciated that she could choose to nurture her own spirit instead of compromising it in order to meet someone else's needs. At last she had a viable emotional alternative: instead of pleasing others, she would look after herself.

## 37

## *Winning Means Losing*

Whilst Gail was damaging the integrity of her spirit by the need to please others, I was soon to meet a young man who was doing so for very different reasons.

Ewan came to work with me as part of a leadership development programme his company were sponsoring. He was ambitious and had been singled out to join the 'high potential' list of the organisation where he was a senior manager. He exuded positivity and enthusiasm and was clearly liked and respected within his peer group. Colleagues deferred to him consciously and unconsciously for approval and support, and he enjoyed that. I noticed that he was a good listener, too, and not afraid to take on board other people's ideas or advice. Although he was a willing participant in the programme he hinted that he wouldn't have that much to learn about leadership or how to motivate a team, his career was going places.

Ewan was first in his small working group to step forwards to meet the horses who would be their learning partners for the day. He strode into the field, marched right up to Charlie and Pebbles, stroked them and then walked back to the rest of the group who were standing at the paddock boundary. It was all over in a few minutes. The horses hadn't moved away from him, but I saw that they both shifted their weight in readiness. Their stance suggested a watchful wariness.

'That was easier than I thought!' he beamed, rubbing his

hands together and looking sideways over his shoulder at the other group who were working with different horses down the hill. 'What's taking *them* so long? We're motoring! Who's next?'

'Before we move on, Ewan, I'd like to check in with you.' I interjected. 'What do you understand the task to have been, and how well do you feel you accomplished it?'

'It was to establish rapport, wasn't it? I think it went really well – I stroked both horses and they looked pretty chilled.'

I thanked him for his response, and invited feedback from the three colleagues who had been observing his meeting with the horses. They were full of praise for how well he had done. I decided that I would let the process take its course.

The next person went, and it took much longer for him to approach the two horses. He was patient though and took his time to retreat and re-approach, adjusting his behaviour so that each horse became comfortable with him. He was rewarded by an active greeting from them rather than the passive tolerance Ewan had inspired. The other two members of the group followed suit. Their encounter took even longer but also ended in a genuine connection with at least one of the horses. As we filtered off for our refreshments break Ewan's demeanour suggested that he still felt he had been 'best' in greeting the horses in the shortest time possible.

It was then time for the team to halter each of the horses and groom them. Ewan was first again to stride into the paddock. This time Charlie and Pebbles would not let him near. Ewan's colleagues on the contrary had all succeeded in the task, demonstrating the quality of relationship they had established. When we debriefed Ewan was less ebullient, but candid. Perhaps he did have something to learn after all?

'I guess I messed it up pretty badly out there. They

wouldn't come anywhere near me! Everyone else succeeded. I'm feeling rather stupid. I probably shouldn't have gone first again, they probably got the hang of it as the day went on.' Again I felt the right thing was to allow his learning to unfold, rather than challenge his assumption.

The day continued as did the same pattern between Ewan and the horses. Eventually, one of his colleagues haltered Fay, a chunky grey mare, so that Ewan could have a turn at leading her. She was not impressed with him though and put her ears back when he tried to guide her to where the grooming brushes were waiting.

### *Redefining success*

'What has really mattered to you about the work you have done today with the horses?' I asked the now crestfallen man.

'I guess what mattered to me was doing well.'

'Is that all?'

He paused and looked down at his feet before replying. 'If I'm honest, no, simply doing well isn't enough for me. I also have to be the best. I have to win. It's been really hard seeing everyone else do so much better than me.'

'And what is it about being the best, about winning, that is so important?'

'Well, if I am not the best, not winning, then I am losing. Who wants to be a loser?'

We chatted then about winning and losing. He talked about how he had been brought up to always be at the top of his class and on the winning team. At school, being the best had been the safest place to be. Having the drive to stay 'on top' was also working well for his career.

'What, today, was lost for you by wanting so badly to outperform everyone else?'

173

He reflected for a moment. 'Well I suppose ironically what I lost was actually the chance to actually BE best. If what you say about horses is true, and they like people who are relaxed, then that is probably why they didn't warm to me like they did to the others. When I'm out to win, I'm quite tense. I guess I'm not really being myself either.'

'So when do you feel you are yourself?'

'Huh? Good question. Not very often. Probably only when I am on my own; when there is no one to compete with. Walking my dog perhaps. I can't even let my kids win at soccer – how bad is that!'

'Is there anything else that was lost today in the need to win? To be better than the rest?'

'Yes. The chance to have something nice happen with the horses. To know that they wanted to be with me, rather than me having imposed myself on them. To have a connection with them, I suppose.' Then he fell silent and a sadness lingered in the space between us. I didn't need to make the link between what he had said and how this insight might have parallels for him at home and at work.

When we rejoined the group Ewan divulged a little of what we had discussed and went on to say that he was going to redefine what winning might mean for him. That success on the programme would be about how much he could learn, and whether he could be himself like he was when he walked his dog. Not only with the horses, but also with his colleagues. For the rest of the day Ewan seemed pensive and took a back seat. Based on the subsequent quality of his feedback to the others I sensed he was observing their interactions with the horses to honour their efforts, not to assess their performance compared to his own.

## *Humility prevails*

The morning of the second day came, and Ewan continued to keep out of the centre of attention and didn't try to take a leadership role or influence the group. He seemed to be doing what he could to help everyone else shine, supporting his colleagues and praising them for what it was they did well. He seemed also to be focussing on the quality of the relationship he could have with the horses not how quickly he could get things done.

After lunch it was Ewan's turn to engage again with the horses and he said he would like to work with Zebedee one of the smaller ponies in the herd. I asked why:

'He looks cheeky. And I guess he is a child's pony isn't he? He might be more used to beginners like me. I'm not going to try to prove anything by choosing a big horse to work with. I'm going to go out there and hang out with him. It doesn't matter if he doesn't come to me. What counts is knowing that he wants to join me. And then for me to enjoy being out there with him.'

Ewan went out into the paddock and took advice from another of the managers who had worked with Zebedee the day before. He didn't walk directly up to the pony but paused a few feet away. He didn't need to wait long for the fluffy white pony to approach, and rub his head against Simon's leg in welcome. Soon the man was walking around the paddock with a diminutive but dedicated follower. Later, I asked what he had changed, what had helped him build this close bond and what he had learned from the experience.

'I let go of the need to win and to impress everyone. Do you know, it was really hard at first, to drop that competitive instinct, but then after a while – wow – it was such a relief to enjoy the experience and not set myself any targets. And look what happened – it was amazing! And the most surprising thing was how easy it was to achieve all sorts of things with Zeb once I had let go of all that.'

## *The power of non-judgement*

As Ewan let go of the need to be better than his colleagues, he not only arrived at an acceptance of himself, but he also found a way to nurture and value his own spirit as well as that of others. When he didn't need to win he didn't need anyone else to lose. And when he didn't need to be the best he stopped judging himself and was able to access his natural energy and creativity. He was also able to find more pleasure in things.

Non-judgemental attitude doesn't come naturally to humans – whether it is ourselves, or others, we form subjective and often undeserved opinions about. For most of us, finding compassion will always be a work in progress because unconscious bias is ingrained in our psyches. This is how our reptilian brain is hard-wired to keep us secure within our own tribe. Failing to recognise our human tendency to judge, and dealing with it, limits our ability to access our own magnificence as a human being as well as value other people. For as long as we judge others, we are also judging ourselves.

Horses, of course, don't struggle with this like we do. They care not how we look, speak, dress or which school we went to. While we humans perfect our mastery of chauvinism with respect to the horse (and the rest of the living world), labelling them as badly behaved, naughty, lazy or stubborn when they fail to do our bidding or meet our expectations in the sporting arena, the horse generously sees us for what we are. For horses face value doesn't count. It is the quality of our spirit, the energy of our intention and what we carry in our hearts that matter.

## 38

## *How Horses Teach us Compassion*

It was a Saturday in early autumn when a herd of horses showed me how transformational true non-judgement can be – for the receiver and the giver. This day, too, was one of the most extraordinary days of my professional life.

We were expectant as we waited to welcome our visitors that day: a group of children and teenagers affected by differing degrees of learning and physical disability. We had been warned by the charity which was sponsoring the therapeutic programme that some of the children were so badly affected by their condition that we might find their appearance shocking if we were not expecting it. The afflictions were indeed hard to see, there was no doubt about it, and bore witness to the suffering the children must have endured over the course of their short lives.

We had planned to manage the introduction of the young people to the herd that day very closely indeed because some of them were not fully mobile. We did not need to be concerned, the horses immediately discerned their vulnerability and took care how they placed their bulky bodies and great hooves. The connection was immediate between child and even the largest of the horses, who all gently and willingly welcomed the newcomers into their herd. The beautiful spirits of these children whose lives were so difficult were what the horses were drawn to, that they were visually different mattered not.

The joy of that day was intense. The gentleness and

affection that the horses showed the children was deeply moving. They trod carefully and touched the small people softly with their silky noses. Verbal communication was difficult for some of the girls and boys, but they did not need words to show their glee as they discovered new sensations like the soft, warm coats under their crooked hands, or the tickling of whiskers and kiss of warm breath on their cheeks. I imagined that while they may not be able to verbalise it, these young people found a new sense of themselves as they spent a day free from judgement, when they did not inspire curiosity, horror or pity. A day when they were accepted and respected *absolutely* for being who they were.

But perhaps what I remember most of all is the happiness of their parents, and the emotion in their throats at the end of the day. I could only imagine how it was for them, at last to have seen their children received and the magnificence of their spirits to have been seen so effortlessly. That, for once, how they looked really was of no consequence.

## 39

# *Following Joy*

## *West Norfolk, 2012*

As the loss of my brother forced me to seek my truth, I could no longer pretend that I was happy in the relationship I was in, regardless of my desire for it to work. Eighteen months earlier, I had left my home in Cambridgeshire and moved to West Norfolk to share my life with the first man I had dated seriously since my divorce ten years earlier. Bestowing my heart again had been difficult but I had been ready to take the risk.

At first it had seemed like the partnership I was yearning for. We had shared interests in the outdoors and when sitting with his three children around the farmhouse table, collecting fruit with them in the orchard or playing party games on dark winter nights, I satisfied an emptiness I had long carried. Happy days I wanted to preserve – perhaps a little too much.

During the months following Gordon's death, our relationship crumbled. We were not strong enough – he to find compassion and love for me in my hour of need, nor me to support him through his own problems. There were islands of happiness – when the children visited, or when we took ourselves away from the house for walks with the dogs. But when at home again, just the two of us, a black fog would descend bringing dark silences and uncomfortable mealtimes. Miles away from friends or family, I felt isolated and acutely lonely. I longed for peace to grieve and for someone to nurture and comfort me. Slowly I accepted that it was not in his gift to give me what I needed at that time.

## *How can I trust myself again?*

If my future was not with him, where was it? And how could I trust myself to decide what to do and where to go having got it wrong? We needed a home: me, my now elderly dogs, the horses and the business. The future felt frightening and I had many sleepless nights agonizing over what to do.

Yet while my personal life crumbled, my professional life took on a new, vibrant shape. During that summer, the client I was meant to be meeting the week that Gordon died had come through with a significant contract for my company, Equest. The work would span 8 months and would need to be based near Swindon, the site of their head office. Through my friend Sarah, I had found a beautiful farm nestled in the soft hills of Wiltshire where I could deliver this programme. It was where she kept her own horses, and as well as all the facilities I needed there I found a warm and caring community created by the couple who ran it. Exceptionally, the generous people who kept their horses at the farm were willing to allow them to participate in the learning programmes we were planning.

Each time that I drove the several hundred miles across the country to deliver one of the events, I would find myself laughing again like I had not done for a long time with the team I had assembled to work with me. The feedback and testimonials surpassed anything I had hoped for from this male-oriented, traditional engineering company. For some, they said it was life-changing work, learning tough lessons but with a peacefulness and playfulness that made it easy. Witnessing the experiences they had with the horses was inspiring for me too. The way they confronted the issues that were holding them back reminded me that I could be courageous, too.

### *Following joy – an easier choice*

Yet still I struggled to commit to a decision about what to do. To leave my partner and his family was too hard a choice to make; I found I couldn't do it.

Eventually, I reframed my dilemma. I would choose to follow my joy rather than leave my despair. That was simpler. That meant that I would go to Wiltshire to live and work, where I had once again been able to step into my whole self uninhibited. Where the rolling hills, laced with mist in the mornings, or golden against the dark sky as the sun dropped in the evening, reminded me that it was good to be alive. I would take action to take care of my soul as well as my business. If I restored myself to full health and energy and gave us both some space to sort ourselves out, I hoped my partner and I would be able to save our relationship. This did not happen, but holding the hope of it helped me to bear my departure.

And so in December, on the coldest day of the year, a large lorry came to take all my belongings from the big farmhouse that I had once hoped to make my home. Later that afternoon, as night was falling, I watched the vehicle grind slowly through the gravel and swing out of the gate which was already disappearing under a blanket of freezing fog. I swung my overnight bag into the boot of my car, wrapped Holly and Milo in blankets and placed them in their crate on the back seat, and set off in the still plummeting sub-zero temperatures. My two faithful companions, devoted and cheerful through every upheaval of the past 16 years, still there, still constant, comforting me now with the sounds of their sleep behind me.

### *The herd migrates*

Our destination was a comfortable detached house I was renting near the farm in Wiltshire where I had been working. I had exchanged character for comfort. After getting unpacked, I took the train back to Norfolk two days later to pick up my horse box and the horses and drove them away to our new life. That day, I was blessed with good driving conditions and a piercing blue sky, and we made good time. It felt like a positive omen. Sitting behind the wheel of my old lorry, cruising towards our new future, the heaviness I had felt was easing. In a couple of weeks, it would be Christmas. I would be alone, but I would be tranquil.

As the low winter sun caressed the hilltops of the Pewsey Vale and gracefully slid behind them, I was leading the horses out to their new paddock to stretch their legs. As they lowered their heads to graze, their breath hung like a mist in the cold air and condensed in droplets on their whiskers. Two red kites circled slowly and majestically overhead against the now pink sky, with shreds of slate grey cloud scattered elegantly here and there like crocheted lace. The tall trees at the crest of the hill stood black and crooked against the sky. Crows cawed their night-time song. Stillness. We were safe. I had done it. The herd had migrated.

I had made this life-changing decision differently. I had accepted that trying to *know* what to do with my mind wouldn't give me answers. The closed cycle of analysis was only serving to make me ill. I had followed the bright light of hope, instead. The choice still brought me pain, but it was easier to make because it connected me with a sense that I was being true to myself. It had taken many years to realise that this could be a much easier way of finding my way in life, instead of anxiously problem-solving and thinking myself into insomnia and indecision. Now I understood that it was when I was joyful that my spirit was able to align me to my purpose. As this personal lesson sank into my soul, it permeated my work in real terms.

## *40*

## *Living the Dream*

### *The wrong job for the wrong reasons*

When he arrived, Neville looked drawn and inside his practical yet immaculate outdoor clothes he seemed somehow flattened. He described how he had felt ill at ease with his team since his promotion into a management position at the retail company where he worked. In his previous role, developing the intranet and employee engagement activity, he had excelled, but now he was feeling out of his depth.

One person in particular was becoming quite confrontational, and he didn't really know how to handle it. The senior management team meetings he had to attend were stressful: he had always felt confident talking about the creative side of his work, but now he had to develop and defend budgets, strategies and resourcing plans. Sometime soon, there was also going to be a reorganisation at the company with a reduction in head count which he would have to implement. He was already losing sleep over it and it was still months away.

'I can see why people think of me as irritable and snappy,' he said. 'Frankly, no one seems to listen to me anymore, so I get frustrated and end up losing it with them. Being tired and worried doesn't help. Then I feel awful, and have to apologise, and the next day find it hard to face any of it.'

Although Neville was an animal lover it was the first time he had been close to a horse, so at first was cautious. In spite of this he was attracted to Winston, the largest in the herd, who took a mutual interest in his new field mate. Perhaps because Winston, like Neville's team, knew he could take charge of the situation easily. And so the process unfolded, the horse leading the man and deciding what happened and when. I called timeout.

'How is it going, Neville?'

'I guess not very well,' he raised a brow. 'Winston is pretty much the boss here. I am feeling useless.'

'What do you want to achieve with him?'

'Well, I'd like to be able to spend a bit of time with him without feeling I was going to get trampled. Enjoy grooming him or maybe taking him for a walk around the field.'

'And what will it take for you not to get trampled? Let's deal with that one first.'

We explored how Neville could keep this half ton of horse out of his personal space. But still he was getting politely pushed around, so I intervened again.

'I don't see much of a change, Neville. I am wondering how seriously you really want to keep him away ...'

'Mmmm. Now that you mention it, I guess I don't want to ... I want to be his friend.'

'And can you be friends while asking him to respect you by keeping out of your space?'

'Well, he might not like me if I push him away.'

'Try it – see what happens.'

### *Needing to be liked*

The next time that Winston attempted to crowd Neville, he waved his arms and jumped up and down. The horse stopped in his tracks and pricked his ears forward, looking at the man enquiringly. Neville burst out laughing. Then the horse slowly, and this time respectfully, approached. Neville was able to stroke him without the horse moving him backwards with his nose.

'That's so cool!' Neville celebrated.

'Well done! Now have a play – can *you* move *him?* And without having to jump up and down? By looking taller? Breathing deeper? Talking louder? Using your eyes?' I challenged.

Neville applied himself theatrically to the task. Contrary to his expectation, the more expert he became at holding the horse out of his space, and moving him with his own physical presence, the more Winston wanted to follow him. Soon he was following at the man's shoulder in the gentle warmth of that autumnal afternoon. Neville's serious, crumpled demeanour had gone.

'It is good to see you having fun like that, Neville.'

'Ah, I don't remember the last time I did. It was probably months ago. Life has become so solemn lately … And I can't believe how being assertive with Winston made him like me more, not less. It's brilliant!'

'Is there anything which feels familiar about this situation, Neville?'

'At work … well … I always worry that if I'm too strict with people they won't like me. But then they take the Mickey, so I get frustrated and cross, so they end up not liking me anyway.'

'So what did you change with Winston to make him not take the Mickey?'

'Well, I was clear about what was OK and what was not. I can't believe it was so easy or that it changed his opinion of me so much.'

'And how clear are you, with yourself, about what you want, Neville?'

He paused and pondered, turning to the horse to place an affectionate palm on his solid neck.

### *Changing isn't failing*

'Actually, if I'm honest. I *am* clear about what I want. I am scared to admit it because I don't really know what would happen ...'

'Say some more, Neville,' I invited.

'Well, I don't really want my job now I've got it. I was flattered when they offered me the promotion. It doesn't suit me in reality. I don't get to write any more or work with the creative team on content or web design. I have to delegate that because of all the meetings I have to go to. Which frankly are tedious. I don't know how I will cope with the forthcoming changes either if I actually have to make someone redundant. Management isn't for me I guess. That's probably why I am so grumpy. Then I feel bad and ingratiate myself on everyone because I think they probably don't like me anymore. Which must make things worse for them; it must be really confusing. It's no wonder we're not getting on.'

'What stops you talking about this at work with your boss if you are so unhappy in the role?'

'Because it feels like failing. And I'd probably get the sack, then how will I pay the rent? And then what will happen?'

'So what will happen if you carry on as you are?'

'Well, apart from anything, I will be miserable. But I will probably get the sack anyway because I'm a rubbish manager!'

### *Laughter: power for the soul*

We turned again to Winston and this time I invited Neville to hold an image in his mind purely about laughter, really tapping into the playfulness he had already found with the horse. They meandered happily around the paddock, running together from time to time, and both finished energised yet relaxed.

We arranged two more appointments during which Neville connected more and more with his impish creativity, which drew Winston almost magnetically. He even whinnied to Neville as he saw him arriving the third time.

For the short periods of time that Neville was with Winston, he was able to rediscover what it felt like to be happy. It helped him to connect with the person he could be when he was doing what he loved and loved what he was doing. At the end of the last visit, we sat in the field with Winston grazing nearby.

'So what are you taking away from here, Neville?' I asked.

'How good it feels to be in my element. I feel so much more confident as well knowing that I can be assertive and say what I want and don't want, or what is OK and not OK, and know that people will respect me for it, not despise me. Like Winnie did.'

'So what will you do?'

'Well, I'm going to talk to my boss about moving out of the management role for a start. And I'm going to get back to doing what I *really* love. That is writing, particularly stage plays – used to do loads at university with the dramatics society. My pantomime was a huge hit, I can tell you. I'll start doing that again in my spare time and see where it takes me.'

For Neville confining himself to an unsatisfactory status

quo had become a habit. But exploring new ideas with playful intent and having a positive attitude to the unknown, can become a habit too. As he learned to flex these problem-solving muscles, the more ready he was to seek change. Six months later, I received an email from Neville. It was titled 'Living the Dream'. He had arrived in New York having been granted a year's career break. He was going to travel and write. I could not have been more thrilled to hear this news.

# 41

## *Healing Through Forgiveness*

### *2013*

Less than a month after my move to Wiltshire, Lorenz, my stepfather, passed away. He was 91 and had been a significant person in my life for 30 years. Losing his stepson and friend had taken its toll and his mental health had deteriorated over the past year. They talked about dementia. I saw an old man grieving the loss of a loved one whom he missed. I was sad and relieved when Lorenz slipped away peacefully. It seemed a strange coincidence that it was a few days before the first anniversary of Gordon's passing.

Now that Lorenz was gone, it was time to fulfil my mother's last wish: that her ashes be scattered with her husband's, in the mountainous region of Spain known as the Alpujarras. This was not only their favourite destination when they explored Europe in their camper van, it was where I had been enchanted by Carabella.

Of course my mother had not envisaged that Lorenz would outlive her by a decade, so, year after year, her ashes had been secreted inappropriately in my French dresser, in a crimson velvet bag, alongside the treasured bone china dinner service that she left behind. Now it was time to lay her finally to rest with the love of her life.

## *My return to Las Alpujarras*

In spite of the appeal of returning to this part of Spain, the nature of our trip left me dreading it. I spent some time, unsuccessfully, researching a suitable sacred place for our ceremony – perhaps a hilltop cemetery or rural shrine. Finally, in frustration, I booked two plane tickets, for me and my sister-in-law Kate, a hire car, and the first decent looking bed and breakfast that came up on the Google search.

The day came to travel. I felt nervous and was grateful to have Kate with me. As we flew over the Sierra Nevada, the cloud beneath us cleared and we saw the contours of the great mountains stretched out below. From above, the peaks looked savage, black with hues of dark green, occasionally dressed with dustings of last winter's glacial snow. Around the foot of the mountains, the quilted pastures and hill terraces of rural Andalucía were greener, neater and more inviting.

I had Mum in my hand luggage and Lorenz was in Kate's. We were surprised at how heavy the bags were and giggled through security, hoping we would be allowed to pass without a search. We imagined what we might say if asked what was in our bags. 'Human remains and a good book, Officer.' Our humour did not mask our discomfort nor the poignancy of what we were undertaking.

Ferreirola, the village where we were staying, lay at the end of a winding single-track road. At the neck of a deep gorge, it was surrounded by wooded slopes which ran steeply down to a river. Many species of tree created a voluminous canopy noisy with birdlife. Higher up, the earth was arid with gnarled olive trees clinging here and there amongst the scree and patches of prickly gorse which I knew would blossom bright yellow in the spring, making the mountainside glow.

Ignorant of my mother's preferred places in the region,

my choice of accommodation had been random. I could not have imagined anywhere so delightful. The rooms, a haphazard collection of renovated farm workers' cottages, were squeezed together around a labyrinth of quaint patios and terraces, all connected with rambling stone steps. Everywhere geraniums and bougainvillaea tumbled creating secret corners and hidden oases amongst the ancient stone.

The brightness of the sun bouncing off the bleached walls dazzled and in its light the azure-blue doors and ceramic pots shone like jewels. We breakfasted in the shade of a vine on fresh bread, fruit, cheese and ham. From the terrace, we could gaze over the gorge at the hillside opposite and take in the astounding beauty of the views encircling us. Goldfinches bobbed and dived and called as they made rich hunting in the warm clean air and in the distance I heard the mellow, musical rhythm of goat bells and the hollering of their herdsman. It was still a world away here, as it had been all those years ago.

As our genial hostess cleared our table I awkwardly explained the purpose of our visit and asked if she knew of somewhere suitable nearby. Unperturbed by my question her face lit up. 'You should take them to the ruined mosque, it's beautiful up there. A truly spiritual place. The Moors, as you might know, ruled this part of Spain once. They chose their places of worship well.' She pointed to a hilltop further up the gorge. 'See that peak jutting out? It's there. You can walk to it in a couple of hours from here.'

Our plan was set. The next day, we would go to the ruined mosque. Today we would buy what we needed for the hike at a local market.

### *Stepping back in time*

An hour's walk away, along footpaths which dissected the

forested hillside, we reached the outskirts of the village where the market was taking place. Before me, the cobbled street passed beneath an ancient stone archway through which I could make out the bright colours and bustle of the rustic trade stalls. Above me a huge bell was built into the centre of the arch. Something potent stirred in my memory ... I had been here before.

The concertina of time collapsed the years and I was riding Carabella in from the dusty trail, weary from the intense heat of early afternoon. That day the square was deserted as its residents took their lunch away from the scorching sun. I had dismounted and watched my horse drink from the huge stone trough which was still there, on my right. It replenished with fresh clear water from three jutting pipes. Then I had led her with the others to a nearby barn where the horses would eat and rest before we in turn sought food, a shower and change of clothes.

I recognised the guesthouse where we had stayed overnight, which had been converted into a café. So Kate and I sat outside, ordered a beer each and soaked in the chattering ambience. I could hardly contain my excitement as I shared my memories with my friend. This no longer felt like something that I was doing *for* my mother. It felt very much like it was something that *she* was gifting *me*. She had brought me back to this special place to reconnect with an experience which had influenced the course of my life so much.

### The resting place

Merchandise at the market had not included sunhats so we bought a silk scarf each as protection from the sun. I draped mine around my head as we set off the next day. We would be the most glamorous walkers on the mountain. As well as our precious cargo and our drinking water, we had what we needed to create a ceremony. I had downloaded Mum and Lorenz's favourite song onto my iPhone; Kate had a poem to read and I a prayer. There were also two tiny rose-crystal angels in my pocket to leave with their ashes.

Our stride and spirit were strong as we stepped out onto the trail. I drank at a spring which trickled naturally carbonated water from the hillside and the smooth, cool elixir danced on my tongue. Here and there enormous cacti stood sentry along the path like Triffids. Ancient, flat threshing platforms which jutted into the valley provided viewing points up and down the majestic gorge with its vast mountains and settlements scattered like breadcrumbs across its slopes.

After two hours hiking the inadequacy of our headwear against the burning rays was evident. We were also lost. When the rooftops and church spire of a rural community appeared in view we diverted to seek refreshment and rest.

Through a doorway shrouded with a heavy bead curtain we found a bodega called Paco's. It was empty apart from an elderly woman, I guessed a relative of the owners, who sat at one end of the dining area watching the news on an old portable television. The patron seemed strangely surprised to have customers asking for lunch. There isn't a menu as such to choose from, I understood her to have said with my rusty Spanish, but she could get us something from the fridge. 'I have ham, cheese, *gambas*, tomatoes, bread, olives, gazpacho,' she reeled off in her gritty dialect. I nodded enthusiastically, '*Si, muy bien, gracias. Y dos cervezas, por favor.*' We chuckled disbelievingly as one huge platter came after the other until our table was completely laden with food. But our feast provided a break not only from the heat but also from the emotionality of our task, the significance of which was only just manifesting to me. When several generations of an ebullient Spanish family swarmed around the next table I yearned to stay and absorb their high spirits rather than resume our journey. I knew it would end with a new kind of goodbye for me.

Equipped now with clear directions to the site of the mosque we peeled off the road by a dirt track which climbed across an arid hillside furnished with flat slabs of grey stone, boulders, pine trees and gorse. Lizards darted off the rocks as our footfall disturbed their slumber. Up we went, and down, and up again, picking our way through scree here, and dense vegetation there, towards the peak where the mosque was concealed. Now that I knew we were close, somehow my legs seemed to ache less. Then a last push through a copse of short stubby trees and barbed flowering shrubs and we stumbled out onto a small plateau in front of the ruined building we were seeking.

### *Close to heaven*

With my back to the crumbling walls I looked around. A universal beauty had unrolled itself at my feet like a never-ending, luxuriant carpet of hazy greys, greens and blues, embroidered here and there with spun silver where the streams and rivers ran. It was as if we were centre stage in this panoramic expanse. Spontaneous tears dripped off my chin. I understood why our hostess had directed us here and why, centuries ago, the Moors would have chosen this as a sacred place to worship. It felt the closest to heaven that I had been in my life, and the perfect place for us to lay our loved ones to rest.

We decided efficiently where to scatter the ashes. I sat down to carefully slip the crimson bag onto the ground before me. Inside the plush wrapping there was a cardboard box containing a thick plastic bag full of grey powder. I had never opened it and somehow had expected something more grand. I looked to Kate who was crouched, doing likewise, downhill of me. Lorenz's ashes were, in contrast, contained in a cylinder which she placed with reverence next to my mother's. Releasing it to reach for her poem, the precious tube jolted into movement. Gravity and the perfectly smooth slope of the rock face ensured a quick descent. In a second, Lorenz was bouncing and rolling down the mountain at a pace.

'Don't worry, I'll get him!' and with a leap Kate disappeared from view.

'It's too late!' I shouted as a large cloud of dust erupted into the air below. 'I'll bring Mum down.' Sorrow and mirth mingling hysterically together, I gathered up our things and climbed carefully down the mountainside.

Lorenz had chosen an even more beautiful spot than we had – a sheltered area at the edge of the incline which was also unlikely to be visited by passing hikers or climbers. Across the narrow valley the acute gradient of the hillside was dissected by an old mule-track descending in a perfect zigzag right down from the upper ridge into the belly. It looked like it had been slashed rhythmically into the rock from left to right and I could see two tiny dots of figures one in red and one in blue winding their slow progress. On my right small boulders formed a low boundary before the land fell away. Two gnarled mountain oak trees bent over towards each other, creating an almost architectural frame for the view which stretched up the line of the gorge.

I looked at Kate and we smiled at each other – there was nothing to be said. My emotion shifted: I was calm and knew it was now time to set them free. To at last say goodbye. My throat was swollen with longing and loss. But then, was there something else, too, in the air? Yes, it was laughter and rejoicing. I could see my mother and her beloved husband in my mind's eye, their arms around each other, swaying to the music they are singing beside their camper van, parked up in the shade of an olive grove somewhere nearby. It was as if I could almost embrace them and join, too, in their joyful reunion.

Immediately in front of the arched trees we placed them and gathered stones to build a small shrine in which we placed the crystal angels. The technology involved to play their song seemed incongruent with the intensity of the moment, but Kate read her poem and I my prayer, then she withdrew, leaving me with them and my thoughts. I tried to imagine what it would be like up there on the mountain during all seasons and at different times of the day. How close it would feel to the stars at night, how windy and cold it might be in the winter months.

A knowing settled in my gut: that bringing Mum here was important, not only for her, but for me too. It was the final act of love that I could offer her, laying her to rest here, in the place of her choosing. By doing so I was also letting go of something I should have a long time ago. I was able at last to find the final piece of forgiveness I needed, for the damage she had done to my relationship with my father and for not being the perfect mother I had once believed in. Instead I was able to simply find gratitude that she had loved me as imperfectly as she had, and what a great gift that had been.

I could have stayed there much longer, finding my peace, but the sky was rapidly turning black all around us. The gathering storm turned the air cold as we scrambled down the mountain and voluptuous drops of rain began to fall the moment we hit the footpath. Retracing our steps from earlier in the day we hurried to cover ground, quickening our pace anxiously as thunder crashed above and lightning illuminated the sky in the distance. By the time we got back to Ferreirola and our new lodgings for that night we were sodden, muddy up to our knees, and chilled through to our bones.

In spite of the damp trail we left across the immaculate tiled floors we were shown sympathetically to our room, and after a hot shower and change of clothes at last I felt warm. Through the white voile curtain which floated at the French windows I could see a pretty table and chairs. I stepped out onto the terrace. The storm had passed by as quickly as it came, and the reinstated sun was steaming the valley around us. I glanced left to find that we had an uninterrupted view of the peak where the mosque lay. I could even make out the inverted 'V' of the arched oak trees, tiny in the distance. The distant clank of the goats' bells and the song of the goldfinches in the pine trees was all I could hear as I stood and gazed away to that distant spot which would be forever in my tender memories.

Later Kate and I raised a glass of Cava to Mum and Lorenz out on the balcony and shared our fond stories. Then we fell into companionable silence each content with our own thoughts. I did not want to move from this spot where I could see their place and feel so peacefully connected with them. I watched the moon rise and the night fall and not until its inky blackness became one with the dark silhouette of the mountain could I tear myself away to bed.

### *Where my horse story began*

When I returned home I was curious to remind myself of the route I had travelled with Carabella, knowing that it had passed through Pitres, the village where Kate and I had shopped at the market. I found the carefully assembled photo album of the holiday in one of my storage chests and made myself comfortable on the carpet, the book placed in front of me. I stroked the hard cover – the prospect of seeing the images inside was to be savoured. The album pages were sticky with age and when I turned the first page it took several others with it.

Oh! the image I was offered jolted me. How could I have forgotten it? There I was leading the nut-brown mare down a steep, rocky mountain track. Instantly, I recognised the sheer hairpin bends that descended the hillside opposite the ruined mosque. I was immediately taken back to how hot I was on that day with Carabella, how my thighs ached and knees trembled from walking the length and incline of the descent which was too dangerous to ride, and how my feet slid on the scree whilst my horse remained solid and sure-footed behind me.

Disbelieving, I calculated that to ride from the bottom of that track to our next destination of Pitres, we would have passed beneath the rubble of the mosque. I had ridden the same route, back then with Carabella, which Kate and I had taken unwittingly with our rucksacks a few days earlier. I had passed, on horse-back, right under the shadow of the rock where lay the shrine.

In the silence of my cosy lounge, the fading photograph in my hands, it was strange for me, the older woman, to connect across those 22 years with her younger counterpart. Bringing the then into the now, and the now into the then. It felt like time had not lapsed at all. It was as if my footsteps and the rhythmic clatter of Carabella's hooves still echoed in the valley where Mum and Lorenz now lay, and their voices echoed and loving spirit danced around me in my new Wiltshire home. My skin tingled as I grasped that we need not be separated at all, by time or by distance.

### Where happiness lies

My mother's last wish had led me back miraculously to the

place where my horse story began: a story in which these infinitely compassionate creatures helped me through dark and difficult times by teaching wisdom, courage, insight and trust. It was a story which brought me closer to who I really am and taught that a happy life hinges on the ability to find joy where there is pain, and to nurture love within ourselves when there is loneliness. And if we are strong enough not to be brave, but befriend and let go of our fear instead, then we can find courage. Then perhaps we can dare to have a big dream, to take a risk, and track towards what is our purpose. Through opening our hearts to the possible and by believing in 'Why not me?' our passion can then emerge, helping us to commit to that purpose. And when we are honest enough with ourselves to let go of what holds us to the past, including resentment and blame, then we can also find peace.

Gazing at the photo of the girl that I was on that mountainside, falling under the spell of Carabella, my thoughts float across the enormity of the intervening experiences I have had. How much I owe to the horses who have inspired, guided, comforted and challenged me at times when I most needed it. The wonder, the pain, the laughter, the liberation; I am grateful for all they have brought me. I know that I am where I need to be, in this new phase of my life, pursuing my goal to share these lessons with others. So that they too will know the wisdom of their spirit, through the wisdom of the horse.

*Dear Reader,*

Thank you for reading *The Spell of the Horse*. I hope you were a little bewitched by the wonderful horses I write about and found their lessons helpful.

I'd love to know what you enjoyed, or didn't, so if you can find the time to post a short, constructive review I would really appreciate that. It is listed on all the main book retailer and review sites like Amazon, Waterstones, Foyles and Goodreads.

I'd also love to hear your own story of how horses have changed your life too. You can reach me on my Facebook, Twitter or Goodreads page, or through my websites: www.pambillinge.com, www.equestlimited.co.uk .

*Pam*

@Pam_Billinge
www.facebook.com/pam.billinge
www.facebook.com/spellofthehorse

## Acknowledgements

My deepest thanks to: Stephanie Zia of Blackbird Digital Books for her patience and partnership; my readers, Kathryn, Neil, Gill, Kate, Lindsay, Justin and Diane for their feedback and encouragement; to Stephanie Hale for her coaching and support through the all-important first draft; and most of all to my partner John, my family and friends who have supported me on the ups and downs of my writing journey.

## *About the Author*

Pam Billinge lives in rural France with her herd of six (one cat, two dogs and three horses). She works to share the spell of the horse through her writing, coaching and therapy work.

To find out about programmes, courses or events where you can learn with Pam and her horses visit www.pambillinge.com and www.equestlimited.co.uk.

## More Non-Fiction from Blackbird Digital Books

*I Wish I Could Say I Was Sorry* by Susie Kelly
*Safari Ants, Baggy Pants & Elephants* by Susie Kelly
*Love & Justice: A Compelling True Story of Triumph Over Tragedy* by Diana Morgan-Hill
*Schizophrenia: Who Cares? – A Father's Story* by Tim Salmon
*Tripping with Jim Morrison & Other Friends* by Michael Lawrence
*Cats Through History* by Christina Hamilton
*Call of an Angel* by Patricia O'Toole

The #authorpower publishing company
Discovering outstanding authors
www.blackbird-books.com
2/25 Earls Terrace, London W8 6LP
@Blackbird_Bks

blackbird

Made in the USA
Las Vegas, NV
09 January 2024